James Blanchard Clews

Fortuna

A Story of Wall Street

James Blanchard Clews

Fortuna
A Story of Wall Street

ISBN/EAN: 9783337018009

Printed in Europe, USA, Canada, Australia, Japan

Cover: Foto ©Suzi / pixelio.de

More available books at **www.hansebooks.com**

FORTUNA

A Story of Wall Street

BY

JAMES BLANCHARD CLEWS

Copyright 1898, by J. S. Ogilvie Publishing Company.

(All rights reserved.)

NEW YORK
J. S. OGILVIE PUBLISHING COMPANY
57 ROSE STREET

INTRODUCTORY.

SHOULD any one feel disposed to criticise this work—and I have no doubt there will be many who will—due allowance should be made for the irregular and hurried manner in which it has been written.

Being a business man, whose time is fully engaged in business matters during the day, it has been necessary for me to do my writing at odd times, whenever an opportunity presented itself. In making this explanation, it is not my intention by any means, to pose as a litterateur; I simply wish to convey the idea that under ordinary circumstances, with more time at my command, my pen might, perhaps, have produced better results.

The story itself (which I have presented under the title of " Fortuna," owing to a vague resemblance of one of the the principal characters to the Grecian goddess of that name) is in a large measure based on fact. The trip across the ocean, with the incidents connected therewith—as portrayed in the first part of the book—is almost identical with one which was brought under my own observation. Some of the discussions, of course, are more or less imaginary and are inserted with a view of furnishing matter, which will not only be readable, but also instructive.

Several chapters have been devoted to " Wall street " speculations and the manner of trading on the Stock Exchange, which is imperfectly understood by the majority of outsiders, notwithstanding that so many of them often have occasion to use its machinery in making investments. One often hears a tirade of abuse directed against " Wall street " by persons who are ignorant of the methods employed there,

INTRODUCTORY.

or else wilfully pervert the facts, in an effort to discredit it as much as possible. There is scarcely any kind of business, which has not its speculative side, and where the element of risk is entirely eliminated; yet one would think, from the wild talk indulged in by some people, that it is confined entirely to " Wall street," and that the latter is without any redeeming features whatsoever. Such talk, of course, is the merest kind of rubbish, for any one with a knowledge of the facts will readily understand the important part " Wall street " has played in floating government, state and railroad securities. But for the services of the Stock Exchange in making a market for the latter, does any one imagine that it would have been possible to build over 1,800 railroads in the United States with a total mileage of 181,000 miles? It goes without saying that the extension of our railroad system—nearly equal now to the total mileage of all other countries combined—has done more to develop and build up the country than any other cause known. From this it will be seen what a great factor " Wall street " has really been in making the United States the foremost nation of the earth.

It is a matter of regret that the practice of injecting large quantities of water in our railroad securities cannot be stopped. This process has made a good many of our securities almost worthless and has been the means of causing severe losses to the investing public, and the discredit attached thereto, has, in a measure been reflected against " Wall street": this, however, is manifestly unjust as the " Watering Can " is not a utensil properly belonging to the " street," but is owned and controlled by the managers of railroads who use it as they see fit. In the pages which follow this introduction, the reader will find an illustration of this, wherein I have given the history of one Albert Stockholm's management of a railroad.

Recognizing the great importance of the Nicaragua Canal to the commercial world at large, and the urgent

INTRODUCTORY.

need of it by the United States in particular, I have introduced a chapter bearing on the subject, in the hope that the American people will realize the importance of the work and lend a helping hand, either by means of private subscriptions or through legislative aid. If my remarks should be conducive in any way toward helping the project along, I shall consider myself amply paid for the time I have spent in gathering necessary data to present the matter completely and intelligently to the reader's notice.

The growing importance of women in the business world has also led me to introduce that topic in my story, and I have no doubt that the majority of the female sex would be quite as capable of managing their business affairs as Miss Montague (the heroine of this book) did hers, if they would only go about it in the same manner.

That Canada will, at some future time, be annexed to the United States, seems quite certain. Already the political battles in the Dominion are beginning to be fought on the lines of annexation. Believing that it would be for the good of both countries to have them under one head, my characters have been led to discuss the subject in a roundabout way, which I trust the reader will not find the least interesting of the various themes presented. In writing a running story I am aware that subjects like this and the Nicaragua Canal are not ordinarily introduced, owing to a feeling perhaps that they do not interest all classes of readers alike. In order to meet that objection, I have written the chapters relating to them in as light a vein as possible, and I am inclined to think that they will prove not only interesting, but instructive as well.

In presenting a story of the times—in which finance always plays an important part—it would be difficult to do so without passing a few comments on the awful panic which lately swept through the land. It is quite likely that some persons will take exceptions to the conclusions I have drawn regarding the causes which brought about the financial storm. If so, I can only say that they have a perfect right to their opinions—as I have to mine.

Before closing this introduction, it may be well to remind the reader again not to expect too much as a literary effort in the pages which follow; there will then be less room for disappointment.

THE AUTHOR.

FORTUNA.

CHAPTER I.

In making a voyage across the ocean from the old world to the new, or vice versa as the case may be, who upon leaving the shores behind has not experienced that quiet but restful feeling which seems to immediately take firm hold of nearly every traveler possessing sea-going qualities? The knowledge that the little worries usually found in everyday business are shut completely out from your existence—that nothing can arise *en voyage* to disturb your mental equilibrium for at least six days—that there is absolutely nothing to do but rest, simply rest carries with it that satisfying feeling nowhere else to be found. All this, providing you are a good sailor and that no urgent reasons exist for wishing you were at home, or on some spot where you could readily communicate with it. Some such reasonings as these were slowly making their way through the imagination of one of the passengers on board a large transatlantic steamer, and although only a few hours had elapsed since leaving Liverpool, he was already comfortably reclining on one of the regulation steamer chairs gazing lazily, first above at the flitting skies, and then down at the rippling waters as the boat slipped rapidly through them. All around him was bustle with more or less confusion, some of the passengers still undecided as to the best means of making themselves comfortable, and therefore standing awkwardly around, while not a few were wandering aimlessly about, with no object in view apparently, so it seemed to the on-looker, although no doubt they were endeavoring to become familiar with their bearings. The passenger first noted while mentally reviewing the delights of an ocean voyage, was not entirely oblivious to his more immediate surroundings, but was engaged in "sizing up," as it were, the human beings who were to be his fellow travelers.

It being the month of September the boat was well filled with the return flow of Americans who had spent the summer in Europe sight-seeing. While engaged in this occupation of "sizing up," his attention finally became rivetted upon a couple seated a short distance from where he was reclining. One of them was a young lady apparently not much over twenty years of age, while her companion's age might have been fifty, or even five years beyond that, as his somewhat set features and dignified bearing made it difficult to guess more correctly. The extreme beauty of the lady was indeed sufficient to attract any one's attention, and in fact, although only a few hours had passed since the ship weighed anchor, she had already received more attention in the shape of glances from her fellow passengers, than is usually allotted to the ordinary individual during a whole trip. It is said that fine feathers make fine birds, and although that is a truism when applied to birds it is often a paraphrase when applied to the dress of an individual. In the present case the young woman's *modiste* had certainly done all that was possible in turning out for her a perfect fitting and becoming gown, but nature had done infinitely more in endowing her with a graceful and superb figure which would have ornamented a dress of the most mediocre description. Nor had nature, which is so bountiful to some and so niggardly to others, stopped there, but as if to show the whole of mankind how perfect a creature it could turn out, when so inclined, it had supplied this being with the most delicately chiseled features imaginable, every one of which bespoke refinement, intelligence and innate goodness. Perhaps the most striking part of her beauty was the delicate tinge of her complexion which contained that soft warm coloring so often likened to the skin of a perfectly ripened peach; and with this was hair to match, of that peculiar but beautiful shade of copperish brown, which is so rarely seen: now add large, dark blue eyes which smiled at you from beneath marvelously long lashes, delicately penciled eyebrows and an absolutely perfect set of teeth, which looked for all the world like bits of polished ivory, and you have the description, imperfect as it may be, of one of the most beautiful creatures that the sun ever shone upon.

The young man first brought to the reader's notice was evidently becoming more and more interested in analyzing the features of the fair unknown, and each moment acknowledging to himself that he had never seen so much loveliness, even in his wildest dreams. Without any intention of being rude or doing anything likely to attract her attention, he nevertheless seemed unable to turn his thoughts or eyes in any other direction. While thus absorbed a hand was laid on his shoulder, and a voice exclaimed, "Hello, Fred! I have been looking all over the boat for you and was just beginning to think you had gone overboard."

The man thus suddenly accosted, immediately sat up, but without in the least betraying his late occupation, and with a slight laugh, replied, "I was just thinking, as you came up, Arthur, of an old German verse, which roughly translated into our mother tongue, runs something like this:

" 'I am, I know not what,
I came, I know not wherefrom,
I go, I know not whither,
And yet, I'm surprised I am so joyful.'

Such a feeling of contentment steals over me, when I am on the water. I seem to lose my own identity completely, and like the wanderer in that quotation, only know that I am joyful, without in the least caring to know the reason therefor. However, to be quite candid with you, I have been studying two different kinds of nature, while sitting here—both of which are incomparable. As we move swiftly along, the glorious skies above with their many tints, and the sun's rays reflected on the water beneath, seem like a never ending kaleidoscope which one never grows weary of watching. That is one kind: quite a different kind, but equally interesting to watch, is that wonderful piece of divinity, talking so animatedly over there with that middle-aged gentleman"—indicating the direction by a slight inclination of the head. "We have visited the Royal Art Gallery in London, the Louvre at Paris and the Vatican at Rome—in fact all the principal galleries in Europe, and you must acknowledge that we have seen nothing in art that can compare in beauty with her. It would be impossible for any sculptor to reproduce her features, and the coloring of her complexion would drive an artist wild in trying to imitate. Her every movement is one of grace. Nature's beauties stand revealed, Arthur. What say you?"

"Why simply this, that could the sedate Mr. Tremaine's New York friends hear him talk, they would say he is learning how to love. *Mon Dieu*," he exclaimed, as he caught a better glimpse of her; "she is handsome though. I wonder who they are? I dare say we shall have an opportunity of finding out soon, and in the meanwhile, time and tide wait for no man which applies equally to dinner on shipboard. Come along. It is time we were making ourselves presentable."

The foregoing conversation was carried on between two young men, both apparently about thirty years of age. They were decidedly prepossessing in appearance—their well-built figures being clothed in fashionable and becoming garments, and from their general make-up and easy bearing, it was quite evident they were used to, and frequented good society. It is my intention to give a full description of these gentlemen later and a very short one here, in consequence, must suffice. They were both Americans—bearing the names of Frederick Tremaine and Arthur Caldwell—and were on their way home, after an absence of some three months, hurriedly spent in visiting the principal places of Europe. As denoted by their conversation, they were intimate friends, and their remarks to each other should be viewed as simply good-natured gossip. Mr. Tremaine was inclined to be reserved, and rarely indulged in light talk; but his friend was of a different mould, possessing a vein of humor which usually asserted itself on the slightest provocation, and which was sufficiently infectious to drive dignity to the winds. This explanation, concerning two of the important personages in this book, is given thus early, in order that the reader may not accuse either at the start of cretinism in any degree; a perusal of what follows will prove that they are both sensible men.

As the two friends were passing in front of the subjects of their conversation, the one called Arthur, whispered, "that is General Montague, Fred," and stepping up to the person so designated, said; " how do you do, General. I had no idea you were on board. Permit me to introduce my friend, Mr. Tremaine." General Montague shook hands cordially with each, at the same time expressing satisfaction that they were to be fellow passengers, and then introduced his niece, Miss Montague.

The whole thing was done so quickly, and was such a surprise to Mr. Tremaine, he could do no more than utter a few words, expressive of the pleasure it afforded him to meet General and Miss Montague, and it was a minute or two before he recovered his usual equilibrium of mind. Mr. Caldwell, however, being an old acquaintance of General Montague's—and besides possessing more than the usual amount of *sang froid*—proceeded to make the most of the opportunity, with the result that in a few minutes he and Miss Montague were conversing and laughing like old friends. Mr. Tremaine and General Montague, both being

"Wall street" men, also foundy plenty to say to each other, but the ringing of the dinner bell soon cut short their conversation. It being their first meal on shipboard, they were naturally anxious to be prompt in taking possession of their seats, so as to avoid any possible confusion—they therefore separated with renewed expressions of pleasure at their opportune meeting, and with a wish, uttered by General Montague, that they would see a great deal of each other during the voyage.

After leaving the Montagues, Mr. Caldwell explained to Mr. Tremaine that General Montague was the senior member of the banking firm of Montague Bros. & Co., one of the richest and best known firms in existence, which transacted business in all parts of the civilized world, having their own houses in New York, London and Paris.

"I became acquainted with the General," he said, "a number of years ago, shortly after I left college. The general and his brother Edward—who I take it must have been Miss Montague's father and who died three or four years ago—were mutually interested with my father in a western land deal, in which they all had considerable money invested. I thus became acquainted with both brothers, as I was brought into almost daily contact with them owing to the fact that my father was in ill health at the time which made it necessary for me to look after his affairs. After my father's death I disposed of his—or rather my interest in the land deal, as he left everything to me—to the Montagues' for $500,000, and a big simpleton I was for doing it as the property was afterward sold to an English syndicate for something like $10,000,000. In justice to the Montagues, however, I ought to add that they tried their best to dissuade me from selling and stated that the property would eventually become very valuable. It seems that it contained coal and iron mines, which since then have been fully developed; and the route for a railroad was projected to run through our tract of land, which of course, gave it an additional value. I don't know whether the Montagues knew of all this when they purchased my interest, but one thing is certain—they made a good bargain and I a very poor one."

"If you have any doubt on the subject, Arthur, I shouldn't think you entertained very pleasant feelings toward the General. What did your father originally put into the thing?"

"Oh! as for that part of it, I suppose I fared well enough. Ten people originally went into the scheme, each putting in, I believe, $30,000—or $300,000, in all; but one by one seven of them dropped out—my father and the Montague brothers buying their shares at about cost—in some cases more and in others less—so that finally those three owned the entire property."

"Your father's one-third interest then cost him just $100,000, which you afterward disposed of for $500,000, so that you realized four hundred per cent., from your original investment, beside your original capital. Not a bad speculation that, it seems to me; wish I could strike something of the kind. But tell me, why were you so anxious to sell?"

"I really can't tell you, Fred. I suppose because I was a simpleton. I figured it out just as you have. I should not have cared so much if the whole scheme had not originated with my father, who really let the others in on the ground floor. However it is past and gone and I had really forgotten all about it, until it was recalled to my mind by meeting the General. Nevertheless it is galling to think what an idiot I was. Ah! well, (heaving a sigh) it is too late to cry about it now, but such an opportunity don't come twice in a lifetime. Thank goodness I am fairly well fixed financially as it is: still I should prefer to be a multi-millionaire. Speaking of the latter, Fred, if Miss Montague is a daughter of the late Edward Montague, she must be worth a great many millions. Edward was the senior partner and accumulated a very large fortune. When his will was probated his estate was valued, I think, at $50,000,000, and since then at least $5,000,000 in interest ought to be added, as it was invested in the best kind of bonds and mortgages. He left his whole fortune absolutely to his daughter—who was his only child—to do with as she pleased, when she reached the age of twenty-three years. I should say she is about that now, but you, of course, are a better judge of that than I, as you have studied her so minutely."

"Nonsense, Arthur. You know perfectly well that I was only joking, with a view of killing time. Besides it seems to me that you, if any one, are entitled to find grace in the young woman's eyes, as her near relatives fleeced you (unintentionally no doubt) out of nearly three million dollars. Her marriage to you therefore would " laughing, " seem like an act of restitution."

"No; no, Fred. You discovered her first, beside so much wealth would be a burden, especially when she gets her uncle's $25,000,000—which she is sure to do, as he is an old bachelor. Now you are just fitted for such a position. You are one of those cool, dignified, intellectual fellows, who knows a great deal about finance and would be therefore of great assistance to her in looking after her investments."

"Judging of the little I have seen of her, Arthur, I should imagine that she is, or will be, quite capable of managing her own affairs. If she inherits the business ability of the Montagues she will do it to perfection. But come, while we have been gossiping here, like two school girls, the other passengers are eating their dinners."

CHAPTER II.

The foregoing chapter has but imperfectly made the reader acquainted with Frederick Tremaine and Arthur Caldwell—two of the important characters in this story—a short biographical sketch of each, therefore, is in order.

Arthur Caldwell—or to give his full name, Arthur Dinsmore Caldwell—passed in the business world as one who was born to have a good time without any particular ambition to become greater. He was the only child of parents who fairly worshipped him and who did everything they could to strew his path with roses. When he got old enough to enter college he was permitted to go his own gait, as his father said he did not believe in hampering a young man who possessed such good traits of character, and he was sure that if left unbridled his boy would keep in the straight road, rather than follow a crooked path. Mrs. Caldwell also had great confidence in her son; and although she gave him good counsel from time to time, she never interfered with his movements, and if he was late in reporting for bed sometimes she took it for granted that he was not getting into serious mischief. So much indulgence on their part might have proved disastrous to some young men similarly situated, as Arthur was kept liberally supplied with pocket money at all times, but it is proper to say that young Caldwell was worthy of the confidence reposed in him, and although he managed to have a good time he never did anything that could be considered very wrong. Before entering Yale he was sent to a high-school, so as to be better fitted for his Yale examination, and it was here that he first met Frederick Tremaine. The young men took a mutual liking to each other from the start, which ripened into warm friendship as the days passed. Young Tremaine was one of those evenly balanced individuals, who went to school for the purpose of getting all he could out of it, and as a natural consequence, stood at the head of all his classes. He was also one of the best all-round athletes in the school, so that he stood high in the estimation of both teachers and pupils, and was liked by everybody for his sterling qualities.

Young Caldwell was no less a favorite with all whom he came in contact, although it is safe to say that he commanded a higher position in the estimation of the students than he did in that of the professors. The reason for this was doubtless due to the fact that he was less of a devotee to his studies, than he was to football and other college games. However he managed to keep fairly well up in his classes and when Tremaine received his diploma he was also presented with one. The young men at that time were between eighteen and nineteen years old—both good looking, well-built fellows, measuring, probably five feet nine or ten inches in height, and as I said before, universal favorites—but here the similarity ended. Tremaine could hardly be classed as a brunette, although he was somewhat of that order; while Caldwell was quite fair and in all respects a blonde. As to character Tremaine possessed a stronger and more evenly balanced mind and had more " stick-to-it-iveness " in his composition than young Caldwell, which would naturally place him on a firmer footing to wage warfare in life's early struggles for an independence. A good part of this was due, no doubt, to the difference in their respective positions. Caldwell had been brought up in the lap of luxury and with the knowledge that what belonged to his father would sometime or other fall to him, whereas Tremaine's expectations of what the future had in store for him were based entirely on his own exertions. He therefore had an incentive to work—which the other lacked, as his future was already provided for—and he intended to keep on working and to spare no effort which hard work would accomplish in winning him a position in life. Tremaine's father had been a cashier in a New York bank for upward of twenty years, and although he received a fair salary he managed to spend the greater part of it as it came to him, in keeping up appearances for himself, wife and son.

Fred would have liked to receive one of the higher college parchments—as he was a great believer in education—still he was satisfied to commence his business career at once. Perhaps he did not realize it, but the faithful work he had put in at school had given him a much sounder education, for business purposes, than that possessed by a good many students graduating from the great colleges.

Arthur's plans were made to enter Yale at the beginning of the new term, but as that was several weeks off, he intended going south first, with a party of friends on a hunting expedition, and tried to induce Tremaine to accompany him. Fred's father, however, was averse to this, as he had succeeded in finding a position for his son in the office of a well-known Wall street banking and brokerage firm which he was anxious that Fred should except at once. As the opening was a desirable one, young Tremaine, of course, acquiesced in his father's wishes, and a week after leaving school he was in harness, performing his new duties. The young men saw little of each other during the next few years, excepting when Arthur returned home at vacation time, and even then the meetings were not frequent, as Fred was engaged during the day at business, and spent a good many of his evenings attending lectures, or in some other pursuit calculated to enrich his mind. Like most Wall street beginners Tremaine had to commence at the foot of the ladder—his first duties being to deliver stocks and bonds at the different offices on the "street," and as he had also to deliver messages and run errands his position was really that of a messenger boy. He, however, found no fault with his work, and as he performed his duties in a faithful and intelligent manner he was soon singled out for promotion. By gradation and on the score of merit he was advanced through the various departments of the firm, until, at the end of five years he was given a branch of the main office to manage. Like most young men on Wall street, the height of his ambition was to become a member of the New York Stock Exchange, but as seats were worth twenty-five thousand dollars each, it was difficult to see how his dream was to be realized. The "branch" he had been put in charge of was one of those offices which was little more than self-sustaining, but the firm kept it open in the hope that some time or other its business would increase—as it was situated in a rather good locality. They had been hoping this ever since the branch was started—fully ten years before—and had changed their managers several times in the interim, but for some reason or other its business failed to grow.

Finally the manager resigned and as Frederick Tremaine's aptitude for business had shown itself in many different ways, the firm felt convinced that he, if any one, could make it a success; he was accordingly placed in charge. Tremaine's appearance had not changed much since he left school five years previous, except that he was a trifle heavier and now supported a becoming moustache, which gave him a more dignified and manly bearing. He had studied hard in the office, and had never missed an opportunity out of it to increase his knowledge of finance and all matters appertaining thereto, with the result that at the age of twenty-four he was more proficient in financial learning than thousands who had been actively engaged in business all their lives. When he took charge of the branch office, he was determined that he would make it a success, if such a thing were possible, and to that end he worked untiringly; and in less than six months his employers had reason to congratulate themselves for placing the office under his control. Business, which had been slack there before, now kept on multiplying until at the end of the year Tremaine's branch showed an average of two thousand shares of stock a day, whereas two hundred shares was above the average when he took charge of it. The manager's salary on this showing was naturally a good one, and as Fred continued to live economically he succeeded in adding considerable to his bank account, until at the end of ten years from the time he entered Wall street as a messenger boy, he had saved something like fifty thousand dollars. It should be explained, however, that a portion of this—at least half—had been made from judicious investments in real estate and railroad securities. A purchase of some Harlem lots at low figures had shown handsome profits in a comparatively short time, owing to the fact that the city had cut a street through the grounds adjoining. An investment in some railroad shares also showed quick results, so that Fred was now in a position to purchase his long-coveted seat in the New York Stock Exchange and start in business for himself. His capital after paying for his membership, would, of course, be small, but his father—who had accumulated, by this time, twenty thousand dollars—had arranged to go in business with him under the firm name of Frederick Tremaine & Co. Fred was quite willing that his father's name (Alan) should figure instead of his own, as the title under which the new firm would launch out; but this Tremaine, senior, would not listen to, saying, " My boy, in the first place you put twice the amount of capital in the firm that I do, and in the second, you are a much younger man, and in all probability will live years after I am gone, so that in time to come you will naturally want to see your own name on the window instead of one which belonged to an individual who has passed in his chips. Beside that, I am not sure that you don't know a great deal more than I do—one thing is certain, you have saved fifty thousand dollars in ten years while it has taken me forty years to save twenty thousand. You are clearly entitled therefore to all the glory there is in the name."

Such arguments Fred felt were unanswerable. So Frederick Tremaine & Co., it was.

CHAPTER III.

Frederick Tremaine found no difficulty in having himself elected a member of the New York Stock Exchange, as he was proposed by his former employers and seconded by Arthur Dinsmore Caldwell. The latter had joined the Exchange four years previous, a year or so after leaving college, having first made a rather extended trip through Europe, accompanied by his father who required a change of scene, owing to the death of his wife. Mrs. Caldwell had contracted a severe cold while attending the annual Horse Show at Madison Square Garden, which developed into pneumonia and shortly afterward terminated fatally. The death of his wife, to whom he was devotedly attached, gave Mr. Caldwell's nervous system a severe shock, and resulted in placing him permanently on the invalid list. The trip to Europe was planned for his benefit in the hope that a change of scene would restore his health : and the trip did seem to do him good, but this new gap in his life was of such a deep and irreparable nature, he was unable to pick up his strength, and a few months after he returned home, Arthur was parted from his remaining parent, who was laid to rest by the side of his beloved wife. The loss of mother and father, who had been so good to him, following so closely one after the other, was naturally a severe ordeal for Arthur to combat, and for a time it seemed to him that life was hardly worth living for, and that a place beside his parents was more desirable than anything else, but gradually time, the healer of all wounds, brought, little by little, drops of comfort to his troubled heart, and as the days went by he became more resigned. Fred Tremaine at this time was of great help to him, and the friendship between the two men, which started when they were boys, became stronger than ever. The gloom of death in a house of mourning is one of the most difficult things to dissipate, and hangs like a pall around those bereaved. Fred therefor persuaded Arthur to take up his abode for the time being with him. Mr. and Mrs. Tremaine were both hospitable people and as Arthur knew he was a favorite of theirs he readily consented—dismissing his own servants and closing his house. In his will Mr. Caldwell bequeathed his entire estate to his son which, when settled netted very nearly one million dollars. Arthur was therefore well provided for and had sufficient to live on without devoting his energies to business. Fred, however, believed every one should be engaged in some form of work and presented the matter to Arthur so forcibly the latter was soon won over to his way of thinking. Fred's thoughts were naturally on the New York Stock Exchange, inasmuch as it was his intention, sooner or later, to become a member of that body himself, he therefore suggested to Arthur the desirability of his buying a seat and taking his chances with the "bulls and bears." This proposition coinciding with Arthur's ideas was soon carried into effect and a short time afterward he was duly elected one of the "eleven hundred." As Caldwell had never been engaged in any kind of business before, he found his new life rather trying at first and the shouts of the brokers and their wild antics made him think that all bedlam was holding high carnival; but gradually this feeling wore away, and after he had been pummelled for about a month—first by one member and then by another, until he thought he had run the whole gauntlet a dozen times over—he got accustomed to the new order of things and began to like it. In relating his experience some time afterward he said that he had been obliged to buy a new hat every day during the first week, owing to the fact that the members used them in playing football, but it finally got so expensive he kept an old hat at his office which he donned before entering the board. He got even, however, on all the new members who were initiated subsequently, as each was obliged to go through the same programme. There are three classes of brokers on the floor of the Exchange, namely: the commission broker, who executes orders for his clients; the two dollar broker who transacts business for his fellow members and the room trader—who is sometimes designated the professional broker—who trades for himself. To the above might be added the arbitrage broker who buys on the New York Stock Exchange, and immediately sells on the Boston Exchange, or vice versa according to the quotations ruling on those two Exchanges. The same thing is done to a large extent between the New York, Philadelphia and London markets. Caldwell decided to become a room trader, and before many months had elapsed he proved conclusively that he was well adapted for that kind of work. He was quick to catch the sentiment of the board, and although he was generally conservative in his dealings he possessed a sufficient amount of boldness, coupled with pluck and nervous energy to make a good trader. At first he operated moderately; but gradually, as he gained confidence in himself and learned the ropes, he launched out on a more extensive scale until finally he was known as one of the heavy room traders.

It is a difficult matter for a person to be a "bull" one day and a "bear" the next, according to the force of circumstances, but Arthur, strictly speaking, was neither an optimist nor a pessimist, consequently he veered from one side to the other, going with the tide, and in most cases came out a winner.

At the time Fred became a member of the Exchange, Caldwell had been in the "Board" four years, and his name was already familiar to the tens of thousands who frequented Wall street. The slips of the News Agencies daily contained items, such as—Caldwell is bidding the market up, or the market is being raided by Caldwell, as the case might be, and as his wealth was magnified into several millions he was considered a power on the " street," and a number of smaller traders tried to follow him, but it must be confessed with indifferent success.

CHAPTER IV.

FREDERICK TREMAINE'S advent on the floor of the Exchange was followed by experiences similar to those practised on all newcomers by the older members, but as he bore the ordeal good-naturedly, and trading was rather more active than usual—thereby keeping the members busy—he was soon allowed to come and go unmolested. A new member of the Exchange who hasn't anything particular to do in the midst of a busy throng, generally finds time hanging heavy on his hands, and so it was with Tremaine, who was anxious to work, but unfortunately had no orders to execute. His firm being just established he, of course, was without clients, but he made the best of it, and now and then executed a two dollar order for some fellow broker, who had more than he could attend to. He expected in time to get a line of customers of his own, who would give him sufficient business to keep him occupied. In the meantime he was averse to speculating on his own account as his capital was limited and he could not afford to run any risk of impairing it.

Besides he had made up his mind to do strictly a commission business, which, after all, is the safest and best in the end. Fred had no misgivings as to the future, as he felt confident that he and his father between them could work up a good paying business; but like all new concerns it took time to do it. Mr. Tremaine's position, however, as cashier in a bank had naturally brought him into contact with a large number of monied people and as he and his son were both respected and liked they before long had the satisfaction of doing a fair business, which developed as the months passed by and grew in time to considerable proportions. At the end of the first year a larger office was taken, and a year later a still larger one was deemed necessary to provide for the firm's increased patronage. During all this time Fred had abstained from taking a vacation, feeling that his presence was necessary at the office in building up his business, but now that it was firmly established he felt that he needed a little relaxation, as he had worked hard and was run down from it.

As his father viewed it in that light he made his arrangements for a European trip to last three or four months.

The life of a room trader is a fascinating one and so Arthur Caldwell had found it—so much so, that with the exception of a few days off each year, he had remained constantly at his post; he left inclined, therefore, to let the market take care of itself for a while, and as Fred was preparing to go to Europe he concluded that it was a good time to slip away also, and decided to accompany him. The trip across the ocean was carried out as planned, and now after having hurriedly visited all the chief places of interest in Europe our friends were on their way home, and the opening chapter in this book finds them on one of the ocean flyers—shortly after leaving Liverpool—bound for New York.

*   *   *   *   *   *

When the reader's attention was diverted from the incidents related in the first chapter—for the purpose of making him more fully acquainted with the lives of Messrs. Caldwell and Tremaine—the writer was under the impression that a brief sketch of each would suffice: he finds, however, that he has consumed more space than he intended, and therefore not only owes the reader an apology, but the Montagues—who are important personages—as well. A narrative to be succinctly and well told should commence at the beginning and be carried through without deviation, to the end, as a part of the reader's interest is naturally lost in looking backward. In this instance the narrator was unable to follow that rule for the reason that he met some of the characters in this work, for the first time, while crossing the ocean, and did not learn of the incidents connected with their early lives until some time afterward. With this explanation out of the way, we will now turn our attention once more to our friends on board the steamer.

CHAPTER V.

When Fred and Arthur entered the salon they found the passengers all seated and the dinner well under way. Two seats together at the captain's table were unoccupied, having been reserved for them. Arthur noticed that Miss Montague's seat was situated next to the vacant chairs, and anticipating Tremaine's wishes, perhaps, he whispered "take the stool next to her, Fred, and I will guarantee that every dish set before you will taste as though it were prepared by Delmonico's chef." Nothing loath, Tremaine took the seat designated.

"We are rather late, Miss Montague," he said, upon sitting down, "and I suppose we owe our host, the captain, an apology."

"Yes, you are somewhat late, Mr. Tremaine," she replied. "Mealtime always comes to me as a relief, as it breaks the monotony of ship life, and as I am generally a good sailor you will learn that I am punctuality itself when each meal arrives."

"You are one of the fortunates, then, Miss Montague," —observed Arthur—"in not being obliged to succumb to the ocean foe. Mr. Tremaine and myself made a good record, in that respect, coming over. As we have been thrown in such good company at the early start going back—we shall have an extra inducement to keep well."

"Yes indeed," laughingly exclaimed Fred, "and I am willing to pay any forfeit you may name, Arthur, if I too, am not punctuality itself, during the entire voyage going back."

"It is not well to boast too much," said Miss Montague, "of what we will or will not do on shipboard. I remember my uncle—the first time he crossed the ocean—made up his mind that seasickness was simply an hallucination which any one could avoid by preserving a stout front and taking plenty of open air exercise. He proved to his satisfaction, however, that something beside that was required, and I am inclined to think he would give almost anything to find out what that something is."

"What did you say, Helen?" asked General Montague, catching the sound of his name.

"I was remarking, Uncle Charles, that you did not always find comfort on board ship, taking one of your recent experiences as a criterion."

"No," responded the General, "I am sorry to say I succumb upon the slightest provocation. I did think at one time (before I had tried it) that I would make a good sailor, but that idea has been thoroughly exploded. I pity the sick—because I am generally one of them, and envy the well, because—ah,—because I don't belong to that class. I must confess I feel more at home on terra-firma, and if it were not for this young lady, I should be there now. Ah! well "—and the General heaved a sigh at what he anticipated was in store for him—" it may not be so bad this time. Captain "—addressing the head of the table—" are you willing to indulge in any prognostications regarding the weather we are likely to experience this trip? My young friends here "—waving his hand in the direction of Fred and Arthur—" are prone to seasickness and are anxious to know what the barometer portends. Give them some encouragement if you can," and the general laughed heartily, in which the whole table joined.

Captains of steamships are asked this question so often by some passengers who are really anxious to know, and by others who merely enquire with a view of saying something—that they as a usual thing answer with a gruff " I don't know, sir; you will have to wait to find out," but General Montague's high standing in life was well known to the commander, and beside that he was one of the kind who considered that politeness is one of the requisites of a gentleman under any and all circumstances.

He therefore answered General Montague's question good-naturedly—saying, "General I am sorry I cannot give your friends much consolation; this is the season of the year you know when storms are generally looked for, and although it does happen sometimes that good weather prevails for a whole trip, I would rather take my chances in predicting the opposite." The captain noticed that General Montague's chin suddenly dropped on hearing this; he therefore added,

"Your friends, however, General, must not take my words too sincerely; a little blow makes the voyage all the more pleasant and breaks the monotony of the trip—for some," and the captain laughed. "I remember coming over last time we had two or three days of remarkably fine weather, and one young lady sitting at my table was complaining that she was afraid it was going to last the whole voyage, and for her part she wished we might have a blow just to see what it was like. Well, she had her wish the next day, and I afterward heard her remark to her mother that nothing would induce her to cross the ocean again. So you see it is hard to please every one." The captain here asked to be excused, as he was obliged to go on deck to relieve the first officer. After his departure several of the guests also got up, leaving, in addition to those already introduced to the reader's notice, four others—two ladies and two gentlemen.

The Montagues seemed to be well acquainted with these people, for after indulging in a few words of conversation with them, the general turned to Mr. Tremaine and Mr. Caldwell and presented them, in the order in which they sat, to Lady Constance Grandwell, Monsieur Rémiere, Mrs. Montgomery and Lord Grandwell.

These four people as a party, were on their way to America for the first time, where they intended spending several months in traveling, visiting all the principal cities, even as far as the Pacific coast—and, of course, taking in, among other things, Yellowstone Park with its ten thousand boiling springs and geysers; its many grand waterfalls, deep cañon and rugged mountain peaks—a sight well worth seeing. Lord Grandwell had first met General Montague and his neice at a large reception given in their honor by one of the general's London partners, and had afterward entertained them himself at his town house.

The firm of Montague Bros. & Co., stood so high and was so well known throughout the length and breadth of the land, the General and Miss Montague naturally had much attention showered on them wherever they went: and their stay in London and Paris was marked by one continual round of entertainment, given by people who frequented the most aristocratic and exclusive circles. In this manner the Grandwells and Montagues had seen a great deal of each other, and it was partly through the general, who gave glowing accounts of America that the earl and his sister accompanied by M. Rémiere and Mrs. Montgomery were now visiting that country, although it is within the range of possibilities that Miss Montague's charming society may have had something to do with it—at least as far as the earl was concerned—as he had been rather attentive to her in various ways while in London; so much so, that society, looking through its matrimonial horoscope, had already seen her portrait hanging in the gallery of his ancestors. Perhaps the future would prove it to have been only a mirage—at any rate society took a little more for granted than the actual facts, at this time, warranted.

Lord Arthur Grandwell sprung from a long line of earls who had always held commanding positions and stood high in the councils of the English government. The present earl was about twenty-nine years of age, and a good specimen of the best type of English gentlemen. He was tall and well formed, with good features—hair and whiskers being of a hazel-brown color—and, taken altogether, he was certainly a fine looking man. As he possessed more than the average intelligence, backed by a large rent roll, he was naturally a great catch in the matrimonial mart. A number of anxious mothers with marriageable daughters—and their fathers too for that matter—had tried to capture the prize, but the earl was clever enough to see through their manœuvres and always gave such people as wide a birth as possible—as he did not intend to be plucked before his time—that is to say, before the promptings of his heart showed him a clear road to happiness.

Lord Grandwell had been chiefly attracted in the first place to Miss Montague, owing to her modest bearing and apparent indifference to the admiration she always created wherever she went. Attentions had been lavished on her by lords and dukes—and in one case even by a prince—with a desire of sharing their titles with her: but unlike many of her country women she was not attracted by their high sounding titles, and offered so little encouragement to their advances that most of them gave up in disgust—although a few of them, with less brains than foresight, went so far as to make formal proposals,—with the same result in each case—namely, a declination, with thanks. Miss Montague had seen the evil results arising from some of the so-called, international marriages, and had no desire to jeopardize her happiness for the sake of a title.

The writer would like to give a full and complete description of Lady Constance, but as considerable space has already been devoted to her brother—the head of the Grandwell family—a brief description at this time must suffice—although her charming personality fully warrants a more extended notice. She was twenty-two years old, bore quite a striking resemblance to her brother, except that she was a more decided blonde and was like him in many ways. While not exactly beautiful, or even handsome, yet both those terms were frequently applied to her—

anyway, she was certainly an attractive looking girl, and exceedingly popular among her friends of both sexes, on account of her many good qualities. She was the youngest of three daughters (Lord Arthur being the sole son) and was her brother's favorite sister—a fact which was apparent to all, as he often took her with him in his travels—although in justice to him it should be said that he was a model brother, and treated each sister with the utmost consideration. Monsieur Jules Rémiere was an old friend of the Grandwell family—having been with Lord Arthur at college—and frequently spent several weeks at a time at their country seat in ———shire. He resided in Paris; was an influential member in the Chamber of Deputies and although not over thirty years of age, was considered one of the Republic's most important statesmen. His stature was a trifle above that of the average Frenchman, and he presented a very distingué appearance, his dark beard being cut à la Vandyke, so prevalent among his countrymen. Although not a rich man—in the sense the term is applied in the United States—he possessed ample wealth for his needs and lived in good style. Like the Grandwells, this was his first trip to America, and he was looking forward to it with a great deal of pleasure, as he loved to visit new scenes, and had already seen the most of Europe and Asia, as well as a portion of Africa.

There remains only one other person to mention—namely, Mrs. Montgomery. She was a distant relative of the Grandwells, and as she only accompanied the party as a chaperone, there is no necessity for going into her history. Suffice it to say that she was the widow of an army officer, who had been killed in active service, and as he left her only a moderate income, she accepted the earl's invitation to accompany them, with alacrity. She was about fifty years of age, possessed an amiable disposition, and was always ready to fall in with other people's wishes, consequently well suited to fill the office she had undertaken.

Returning to the salon once more we still find the individuals previously mentioned seated at the captain's table, although it is evident that they have finished their dinner and are merely tarrying for the purpose of indulging in *conversazione*. Presently the General remarks, "Suppose we go on deck and regale ourselves with a good Havana. I have a few left from the stock I brought over with me and shall be glad to share them with you, gentlemen." The General's offer was accepted with alacrity, and while he went to his stateroom for the cigars the others went on deck. Their chairs having been procured for them by the deck steward, they were presently joined by General Montague, who remarked—while passing around the cigars—"what a pity, ladies, you cannot join us."

"Yes, uncle," Miss Montague said, "I agree with you, but mankind, through an organization known to the world at large as society, has long since decided that smoking is one of the exclusive rights belonging to man. On what ground I have never been able to determine, for I am quite sure "—laughing—"I could keep a cigar lighted as well as any one. "If one asks for a reason why women are not permitted to smoke, she is told that it is not a nice habit; that it would not be proper, etc. Now I grant all that, but why then do men indulge?"

"I have often wondered myself at the injustice of the thing," said Lady Constance. "But then the men are permitted to do so many things, which society looks askance at, if our sex attempts to imitate them. I have long since given up trying to solve the problem. Why is there so much injustice in the world, General?"

"I am afraid I cannot explain to your satisfaction, Lady Constance. A long established custom permits my sex to do numerous things which your sex, physically, couldn't stand. Smoking may be one of them. You must recollect, my dear Lady Constance, that you are made of more delicate fibre than I, and what would simply be a nerve tonic for me, would prove to be poison to your delicate system. It is for good and sufficient reasons that women have been debarred from smoking and you had better make up your mind to the inevitable."

"Oh I have long since made up my mind to that"—laughing—"but I asked you to explain why men and women are not on a more equal footing, and in answering my question you confine your argument to the practice of smoking which I, for one, have never had the slightest wish to indulge in."

"Well I told you at the start," answered the General, "that my explanation would not be satisfactory to you. If you were a real philosopher you would accept the wisdom of many generations without trying to learn more. What women complain of most, is that they are not permitted to do certain things, without being censured by society, which men can do with impunity. Now as most of the things complained of come under the category of vice—or something approaching it—it strikes me, that women, instead of wishing to indulge in some things that men do, are a great deal better off without them. Instead of trying to imitate our bad ways, they should shun them altogether and thus set us a good example."

"That is true enough, general," answered Lady Constance, "but you know that 'to err is human,' and that applies equally to both sexes. Do you think a woman should be punished or censured for something she does, which would be entirely overlooked in a man? It seems to me that justice at least demands that both should be treated alike. Yet we all know that the reverse is often the case. Do you think that is fair or equitable?"

"Not at all. Not at all," slowly repeated the general, "but because men have vices that is no reason why women should also have them, and that after all is the question you originally put to me. If it were not for the softening influence of woman, and her innate goodness and purity which are constantly before us as a guide, we men would all go to the dogs in short order. So, you see, women have a noble mission in life, which they should keep before them at all times and in that way they are not likely to do anything wrong."

"I am willing to acknowledge, General, that you have made the most of the subject from your standpoint, but I still remain unconvinced. Mr. Tremaine you don't look like a biased person; won't you give us your opinion?"

Thus appealed to that gentleman laughingly said: "I am always glad to take up the cudgels in behalf of your downtrodden sex, Lady Constance. General Montague has given you a strong argument, but having enlisted in your cause I must find means to combat it." Then straightening up, as though he enjoyed the task, he commenced as follows: "Smoking is only one of many things men are permitted to do, which the other sex are debarred from. I believe that the Lord, in creating man and woman did not intend that one should enjoy greater privileges than the other; nor that it was His idea that they should inhabit this earth on unequal terms. I have read the Scriptures through from beginning to end many times, and there is nothing in them which conveys any such idea. How it is that the male portion of the *genus homo* has taken it upon himself to declare that he can do certain things which woman must refrain from, I cannot imagine. It is certainly a travesty of justice that such a state of affairs should exist in this enlightened age, and I look for the time when such favoritism will be a thing of the past. It is unworthy of a great people and is a blot on the escutcheon of all civilized nations. The name—*woman*—stands as an emblem of all that is good and pure, and if you now and then find one who has forsaken the beaten track of righteousness, you can make up your mind that she has been tempted through the instrumentality of man."

Tremaine's remarks were delivered in an earnest manner

befitting the occasion, and when he had concluded, won decided approval from the members of the sex whose cause he was championing.

"You say, Tremaine," broke in General Montague, "that you have read the Scriptures through from beginning to end and assert that they contain nothing which could be construed as meaning that man and woman were not born equal. I would like to ask you if you found anything which says man shall not dominate? Being usually the stronger force, both physically and mentally, and therefore a naturally constituted leader, it would seem strange if he were to dwarf those superior qualities with which he has been endowed, and allow himself to be led by an inferior force. Since the beginning of the world man has been the recognized leader, and with such a record back of him I am inclined to think he will continue so to the end. One meets plenty of brilliant women, of course, who intellectually, compare favorably with some of our brainiest men, but in the aggregate they constitute only a small minority."

"You only say that for the sake of argument, general; we know you don't believe it," interposed Mrs. Montgomery.

"I assure you, madam," the General replied, "I am very much in earnest. However, we will hear what some of the younger generation have to say. What is your idea of it, Arthur?"

All eyes being turned to Caldwell, he had no alternative but to also express his opinion.

"It appears to me," he thoughtfully began, "that both sides of the case have been admirably handled. Lady Constance from her standpoint has shown that the world-at-large—although not exactly discriminating against the female sex, is apt to condone—h'm—let us say social errors, when committed by a man, which it is not willing to overlook if the offender be a woman. This, on the face of it looks like injustice—in fact it can be called by no other name—but is there not a reason for such discrimination? Tremaine has argued that woman is innately more pure than man, and I am inclined to think that he is right. Taking this for granted, is it not possible that herein lies the solution or answer to the question which Lady Constance has asked, and from which this almost endless discussion arose. We have placed woman on such a high moral plane, several degrees above man, it is natural that a downward step on her part attracts more attention, and consequently more censure from the outside world than it does when the transgressor is a man. Besides the sanctity of our homes requires that woman should be kept as pure as possible, as the young child in its innocence and purity is left almost entirely under her care, and its future is made or marred by her teachings. For that reason we are more exacting where woman is concerned, and consequently expect more of her. General Montague has shown quite clearly that a woman is left untrammeled in her wish to imitate man when her object is a worthy one, and it is only when she stoops to something lowering, that she is pulled up with a sharp turn. I admit it seems unjust that a woman should be censured for some indiscretion she has committed, while a man for a similar offence is allowed to go unchallenged, but in my opinion, it is as I have before stated, because we wish to keep her on a higher plane, and in that she has no just ground for complaint."

At the conclusion of Caldwell's remarks, which were rather serious for him, Lady Constance's face, as well as the others, expressed approval, but as if unwilling to give up so easily the former shook her head despairingly, saying:

"You give very good reasons why the female sex should walk a straight line, but like General Montague, you have failed to show why your sex should be granted immunity."

"You are like all women, Constance," her brother replied. "While convinced against your will, you hold the same opinion still. I am afraid this much mooted question cannot be settled by us."

That Lord Grandwell's idea was also shared in by the others present, was self-evident from their silence. The argument, debate, or whatever it may be called, helped to pass the first evening on shipboard very pleasantly, and what was still more important, it had the effect of putting those engaged in it on a friendly footing with each other.

Presently General Montague complained of stiffness in his joints from sitting so long in the open air, and asked Lady Constance if she felt like making a few turns around the deck.

"With pleasure," she replied, " providing the motion of the boat will permit of it without jostling every one we meet."

They thereupon commenced one of those promenades up and down the deck, which seafarers so much delight in and which is so essential on board ship, as it is about the only exercise a passenger can take. Miss Montague accepted Tremaine's invitation for a similar stroll, and the remaining gentlemen concluded to follow their example—Mrs. Montgomery preferring to go indoors.

Lady Constance's remark about jostling into people had some foundation in fact as the sea had become quite rough, and the boat was pitching not a little, although not to such an extent as to make walking wholly undesirable.

"Do you know, Mr. Tremaine," Miss Montague was saying, "I have enjoyed the evening so much. I only hope that our little coterie will remain well during the whole voyage. Ship life is such a bore unless you have some congenial spirits around with whom you are on good terms. But I had almost forgotten that you and I were strangers to each other only a few hours ago. It is really astonishing, the rapidity with which one gets to know another on a vessel. I often marvel at it, but suppose it is due to the unconventionality of ship life. I like your Mr. Caldwell very much. He has such pleasant manners and seems such a clever man. I suppose you and he are great friends? In days gone by I have heard papa speak of a Mr. Caldwell, in fact a gentleman of that name used to call frequently at our house, but he was much older than your friend. Perhaps he was a relative of this Mr. Caldwell. Do you think so?"

"He was doubtless Arthur's father," Tremaine replied. "I know he was connected in some large business transaction with your father, and presume that he was the person you have reference to. I am glad you like Arthur. He is one of the finest fellows living, and the most loyal friend man was ever blessed with. Everybody on the Stock Exchange likes him—in fact he is a universal favorite with all who know him, and that includes a large portion of both sexes. He and I have known each other a long while, having first become acquainted at school, and the friendship struck up there has ripened and blossomed with each passing year until we are now almost like brothers."

"You are both to be envied," said Miss Montague. "I sometimes think girls do not form such close and disinterested friendships as you find among men. Still I have been abroad so long, isolated from my own people, I have no doubt that is a mere fancy which will soon be dispelled after I have been home a short time."

"Most men—and women too"—Fred said, laughingly—"prefer to form a friendship with one of the opposite sex, and I don't know but what that is the most natural thing after all, but it would seem that Arthur and I have not heretofore found our affinities."

With a never flagging conversation they paced up and down, now and then exchanging a word with General Montague and Lady Constance as they passed them, and occasionally with Lord Grandwell or his two companions. It was evident that they enjoyed the promenade thoroughly, from the fact that they kept it up for some time after the other passengers had gone indoors.

The increased pitch of the boat, however, was beginning to make walking a trifle laborious, and as Miss Montague observed that her uncle and Lady Constance, as well as the others, had disappeared, she thought it advisable to go in. After helping her down the companion-way Tremaine went to the smoking room in search of Caldwell and found him evidently communing with himself, for he said—upon the former's entrance—" I was beginning to think that you were going to allow that young lady to freeze herself to death. The General is commencing to feel a bit squeamish— and has retired to his stateroom,"—then adding, mischievously,—" he left word with Lord Grandwell and myself to keep an eye on you. My co-watcher got tired of waiting and left me on guard."

" Sorry to keep you up, Arthur. I have had a delightful walk and am now ready to turn in. Good-night. I hope our newly-made friends will be able to put in an appearance to-morrow. They are charming people."

" They are indeed," his friend answered; and with an idea of further teasing him, he continued, " remember you have got to get up early if you want to be first in the race. The earl is formidable."

" I am not inclined to enter the race," Tremaine good-naturedly rejoined, " so don't let either your wish or your thoughts have unlimited play. Good-night, again. I hope you will sleep well."

" Thanks Fred, but remember Shakspeare's lines:

" 'She is a woman, therefore may be woo'd;
 She is a woman, therefore may be won.' "

Having had the last word Caldwell disappeared with a laugh.

CHAPTER VI.

Mr. Tremaine's parting injunction to his friend the previous night, had evidently been uttered in earnest, for he was one of those men in whom braggadocio, or anything approaching it, was utterly lacking. He was perhaps over-modest in this respect, but it jarred on his nature to hear any one even joke on matters of that kind. However this feeling did not prevent his thoughts on arising the following morning, from returning to Miss Montague, and his pleasant stroll with her. Neither did it slacken his movements, when he found upon looking at his watch, that only twenty minutes intervened before the breakfast hour, for he was anxious to be punctual to the minute, inasmuch as Miss Montague had asserted that she was always on time. His morning plunge had to be omitted, but otherwise he was able to complete his toilet, and just as the twenty minutes expired, he emerged from his room, and had the satisfaction of entering the salon almost simultaneously with Miss Montague, and to say good-morning to her as she took her seat, and also to the Grandwells and M. Rémiere, who were already in their places. General Montague and Arthur, however, had not put in an appearance, and noticing this, Fred expressed a hope that the General was not ill.

"I haven't heard from him this morning," Miss Montague replied. "After leaving you last evening, I learned from Lady Constance that he was not feeling very well, and I am afraid he is already on the sick list. My poor uncle never feels at home on the sea, although he enjoys perfect health on land, something I can't quite understand."

"It is one of those unaccountable freaks of nature, Miss Montague," Fred answered, "for which there seems to be no good reason. The man who discovers a cure or preventative for seasickness will make an independent fortune, provided he can control the secret, and dole it out in small parcels to the public. If I were a physician I would devote the remainder of my days to study, trying to discover some compound which would absolutely prevent nausea at sea. Such knowledge would be of incalculable benefit to mankind, and my name would be handed down to posterity as the greatest physician of the age. But it is time my friend Caldwell put in an appearance. If you will excuse me for a moment, I will run down to his stateroom and see what is wrong with him, and also make inquiry at your uncle's stateroom."

Upon entering Caldwell's room, he discovered that gentleman still in his berth, apparently oblivious to all mortal or immortal sounds. Upon being wakened and informed of the time of day, Arthur said he must have neglected to wind his watch—an observation under the circumstances which could only come from a man half asleep—as he had not even looked at his horologue since the previous night, and besides, as matter-of-fact, it had been wound up as usual. Fred next directed his steps toward General Montague's room. He found the General propped up by pillows, but evidently not much the worse for wear, as he was eating the first meal in the day with seeming relish. Answering Fred's solicitous inquiry regarding his state of health, the General informed him that he was not exactly sick, but the principal organ of his digestion compelled him to remain quiet for a little while, until he got used to the motion of the boat. He thanked Fred for his call, and asked him to say to his neice that he was all right, and expected to be up and out within an hour or so. Returning to the salon, Fred informed Miss Montague of her uncle's condition, and she expressed her thanks for the trouble he had taken, and seemed to be quite grateful for the information he brought.

Breakfast is not the most enlivening meal on shipboard, and passengers are glad, as a rule, to finish it, and go up on deck where the invigorating sea air seems to infuse new life into them. This feeling is probably due to the fact that they have been shut up in their staterooms for a period of eight or ten hours, and the stuffy air they have inhaled over night, naturally causes a sense of oppression. The rooms on the deck are a marked improvement in this respect, as the port holes can almost always be kept open, and thus good ventilation is insured. Unfortunately for our friends, those desirable rooms had all been taken when they put in their applications,—in fact they are generally engaged six months to a year in advance—consequently they had to content themselves with accommodations between decks. Without wasting time in superfluous talk, the ladies and gentlemen in whom we are interested, finished a substantial meal, and hurried up on deck to bask in the rays of the sun, and otherwise make themselves comfortable. An accommodating steward, after considerable searching, succeeded in locating their chairs, and placed them in a row. Fred's chair, by chance (perhaps design would be a more appropriate word, as he superintended the job) was placed next to Miss Montague's. Instead, however, of immediately sitting down by her side, he excused himself, remembering that he had an important letter to write, which he wished to have mailed at Queenstown, for London. Lord Grandwell, under the circumstances, naturally took the seat next to Miss Montague, inwardly thanking the inventor of letter writing, which compelled the good-looking American to absent himself, even for a short time. He was not easily thwarted in anything he undertook to do, and he had set his heart on making the American beauty and heiress Lady Grandwell, although in justice to him, it should be stated that he was inspired solely by affection for her, and the fact that she was the richest woman in the world, did not influence him in the least, although he fully appreciated the benefits to be derived from great wealth, such as hers. His position in the world was already a good one, but with her fortune added to his he and his wife would be the envy of all England. He had had plenty of opportunities to marry, and to marry well, but the sentimental part of his nature had never been touched deeply enough to call forth a proposal of marriage, until he met Miss Montague. It was easy enough to fall in love with her, she was so beautiful in face and form, and withal so charming, her mere presence inspired it, and all who came in contact with her felt the intoxication to a greater or less degree, without trying to resist the spell,

> "Her overpowering presence made you feel,
> It would not be idolatry to kneel."

Frederick Tremaine was not a man calculated to fall in love with any woman at sight, in fact we doubt if he had ever had a genuine *affaire d'amour;* the reader, however, has heard his exclamations concerning Miss Montague's beauty in the opening chapter of this book, which would seem to indicate, coming from a man of his somewhat phlegmatic temperament, that if he had not already succumbed to the influence of love, he had, on the surface at least, become partially intoxicated, and although he did not realize it, and would have scoffed at the idea if any one had presented it to him—he was in a fair way to become wholly so, by the time they landed in New York, for—

> "She was like
> A dream of poetry, that may not be
> Written or told—more than beautiful."

Lord Grandwell's attentions to the young ladies he had been brought in contact with, had always been received with so much encouragement by them, and their match-making mothers, he could not help but believe that he was a desirable *parti*, and in this he was not mistaken, for he was in every respect, but he realized, as Tremaine's fine figure disappeared in the companion-way, that the much coveted young lady by his side was not to be had simply for the asking, and that there were others in the field beside himself. Some such thoughts as these were flitting through his mind, which in turn were reflected in his physiognomy, for his face, now bore a troubled and perplexed look, which ordinarily was absent. Noticing his pre-occupation for a minute or two without disturbing his thoughts, Miss Montague finally said:

"You appear to be *distrait* this morning, Lord Grandwell. I hope you are not already regretting your trip to our shores. If you are, I shall, as a patriotic citizen, consider it uncomplimentary to America."

Aroused from his reveries by the voice he loved to hear, Lord Grandwell's countenance assumed its wonted expression, and he laughingly replied:

"I have no room for such thoughts as those, Miss Montague. If your home were in Kamtschatka, where I am told the climate is not altogether desirable, I should still be content to follow you."

Although this was uttered in a semi-jocose tone, it was quite plain, from the accompanying look he bestowed on his listener, that there was much more than a grain of truth in his words, and that she realized it, was evident by the slightly increased warmth she felt steal into her cheeks, although no noticeable change in them took place to denote to an outsider that she had taken in their full meaning—for the reason perhaps that delicately tinted roses habitually ornamented her cheeks, which were raved about by men, and made her the envy of all women.

The reader must excuse these lapses into time and remember that the young lady who figures so prominently in this tale was, without doubt, the most beautiful woman in all Christendom—at least her numerous admirers thought so, and we must take it for granted that they were competent and impartial judges.

Miss Montague was now saying to Lord Grandwell—

"If your absent looks were not due to thoughts of America, it is quite certain that they were concentrated on somebody or something in Europe, and as we are leaving the old world behind us, you should endeavor to leave your disagreeable reflections behind also. You must recollect that we are going to the land of milk and honey, where sorrow and trouble never dwell, and where the streets are paved with gold and silver—that at least is the popular impression among emigrants when they leave their old homes."

"No one can ask for more than that," Lord Grandwell said, with a smile. "If I can find a country where sorrow and trouble never dwell, I shall be willing to foreswear my allegiance to the queen, and take up my abode in that haven of rest. I am afraid, however, such visions are of the Utopian order and few ever realize them. You have heard the old saying that

"'Distant hills are green,
But when you get there,
There is nothing to be seen.'

"I dare say a great many poor, deluded creatures set out for America, expecting to find the lost Paradise. In such cases I should imagine that my quotation or something like it must strike them forcibly. Building air-castles is a pleasant occupation while it lasts, but the realization afterward that their foundation consisted of nothing more substantial than rose colored imagination must be bitterer than wormwood to swallow, and is apt to sour one's constitution for a considerable time."

"One would imagine by your observations, Lord Grandwell, that sometime or other you had been engaged in some such pastime," Miss Montague laughingly rejoined, "and that wormwood was sweeter than honey in comparison with what you really swallowed. Tell me all about it, won't you? Perhaps I can prescribe an antidote."

"Not now," the earl replied. "My castles have not reached the proper altitude yet to admit of their durability being tested. I am afraid shatteration—is that an allowable word?—would follow if I obeyed your behest, and I am not willing to run that risk until I have reason to believe fortune favors me. I can only hope that my architectural plans will meet with your approbation when they are laid before you."

Miss Montague must perforce have been accused of obtuseness, if the earl's meaning had not been perfectly plain to her. That she understood was quite apparent, for she slowly said, "Erecting castles in the air, Lord Grandwell, is after all rather unprofitable for the builder, unless they have something substantial to rest on. I confess I have several times tried it, but somehow the structures have generally been so frail, 'shatteration,' as you call it, soon follows. But here come my uncle and Mr. Caldwell—the invalids of our party. Good-morning, Uncle Charles. How do you do, Mr. Caldwell. I congratulate you both on your escape from thraldom. I rather expected my uncle would surrender—but you, Mr. Caldwell—after your protestations last evening—surprise me. Your solemn remarks of last evening were evidently too much for you. Take my advice, don't try to digest anything so weighty again. They really gave me the nightmare. I saw nothing in my dreams but fantastic shapes of you, in all kinds of powdered gowns and ermine wigs, but each time you disappeared and nothing remained but smoke."

"I rejoice to think, Miss Montague," Arthur replied, "that I occupied a portion of your dreams, even though I did not appear in my customary shape or dress. I hope however that there will be no disappearance in the future —keep me in your thoughts constantly and I shall be happy for the balance of my life."

All present laughed, especially the General, who said, "How comes it, Caldwell, that you were on the sick list? I thought you were water-proof and copper-lined which rendered you impervious to anything like seasickness— which Mr. Tremaine elegantly styles 'nausea at sea.'"

"I am so far, General. My sickness is a phantasm produced from your niece's dream-troubled brain. Rarebits late at night are bad for digestion."

Presently the captain passed and informed them that they would soon be at Queenstown, and if they had never been in Ireland they had better go ashore. As Lord Grandwell and his sister were the only ones present who had visited the "Emerald Isle," the captain's suggestion was considered a good one, and the whole party an hour later, boarded the tender which came along side, and were shortly afterward landed in the country which wishes to dispense with the protecting arm of England, a result which Gladstone tried so hard to accomplish.

Who has landed on the Queenstown wharf who has not been importuned to select a genuine black-thorn stick from a great variety of all sizes and shapes offered for sale? Or has not been surrounded by a score or more of venders anxious to sell you a beautiful Tam O'Shanter of a verdant hue? This familiar scene seldom varies, and on this occasion was still the same; but our friends had no idea of purchasing anything they could carry away with them, except that which could conveniently be stowed away in their memory. At the suggestion of Mr. Caldwell, they engaged a couple of jaunting-cars to take them for an hour's ride, by which time they had to be back to board the tender returning to the ship. Miss Montague and Mrs. Montgomery, with Lord Grandwell and Mr. Caldwell, occupied one car, while the other members of their party filled another. The ride was made without any noteworthy incident transpiring, although the novelty of the thing and the fact that each was in a mood to enjoy anything, made the trip a pleasant one.

The usual pack of ragged urchins accompanied the carts during the greater part of the voyage, and to the tune of English sixpences, pennies and other odd bits which our friends good-naturedly dropped on the road side, they were treated to a great variety of gymnastics which did the little chaps credit, and which, considering their diminutive size, would have ensured any one of them a first-class engagement with Barnum's circus. Poor little tots, they worked hard and fully earned the pieces of money that were thrown to them, although, as Caldwell remarked, "their early gymnastic training would be of incalculable benefit to them when they emigrated to America and joined the metropolitan police force, where so many of their national relatives are to be found." Perhaps the hardiness of the New York police is due to some such early training, for certainly no finer body of men, taken as a whole, can be found anywhere —not even the "Queen's Own," of which the average Englishman is so proud. The most lasting thing which clings to one's memory in connection with these Irish rides, especially when the horse can be induced to assume a gait more rapid than a dog trot, is the shaking up one constantly receives, and which calls forcibly to one's mind the fact that one is really on a jolting car. However, as General Montague remarked, "it was a direct aid to nature in digesting something that was indigestible,"—whatever that meant. Each member of the party seemed to have thoroughly enjoyed the little trip; and the incidents connected therewith—although of a simple nature—afforded considerable food for merriment, even after they had returned to the ship. How little is required to make pleasure when a person is in the mood for it; and alas! how much,—when a person is not.

CHAPTER VII.

"Do you really think, Grandwell, that Ireland is better off without home rule and that Gladstone's efforts will prove futile?"

The question came from M. Rémiere, who with the balance of our party were lingering over their dinner on the second day's voyage. The trip to Queenstown had brought the subject of Ireland and her woes to the surface, and the existing relations between England and Ireland—ruler and ruled—had been vigorously discussed during the meal. M. Rémiere and the Americans, being citizens of Republics, sided with the "under dog" as Caldwell facetiously styled Ireland, while the earl—as a peer of the Realm—and his sister, naturally contended that their government's policy was proper and just.

In reply to M. Rémiere's question, Lord Grandwell said, "I most assuredly do, and furthermore I believe that Mr. Gladstone made the biggest mistake of his life in advocating home rule for Ireland. Instead of his long and honorable career ending in a blaze of glory, his biographers will have to chronicle the fact that the chief policy of his closing administration failed of accomplishment."

"Granting what you say is true, Grandwell, don't you think the poor people of Ireland should be permitted to govern themselves if they want to?" persisted M. Rémiere.

"If the sentiment in that country for home government were unanimous," the earl replied, "I don't think there would be any great objection; but you must understand that the best educated, and therefore the most enlightened people—those in the north of Ireland—are opposed to home rule."

"But why?" asked Miss Montague. "One would naturally suppose that the idea of self-government would stir up a patriotic feeling in the bosom of everybody concerned."

"Quite right," the earl answered; "and if that feeling alone influenced them, the sentiment would be unanimous for home rule. But, unfortunately, there are a great many people in Ireland, constituting a majority who are not able to rule themselves, let alone make laws to govern others; their idea of administering public affairs would be something on the order of using their shillelahs freely at all times. I do not say this with any feeling of animosity toward any class of citizens in Ireland, as I entertain nothing but the kindliest feeling for them all, and sympathy for their unfortunate condition; and, not only that, but I always use my position as a member of the House of Lords to do everything I can to better their condition. If the people in Ireland would really be satisfied with some kind of local arrangement, to govern, in a measure, their home affairs, and at the same time permit the English Parliament to supervise them, they would doubtless have their wish gratified; but the great trouble is they are restless under any kind of restraint, and after receiving the first concession, they would very soon be clamoring for full independence, and that, of course, is out of the question. England is to-day the greatest nation on the face of the earth, owing to her large possessions, and she is not knowingly going to do anything which would be likely to lessen her importance in the remotest degree, such as the withdrawal of one of the members composing her united kingdom. Possession of Ireland to be sure is not absolutely necessary for the welfare of England, but cut the string in one place and it might be necessary to do it another. The people in Scotland and Wales are loyal to the heart's core, and perfectly contented with the existing state of affairs, but it is not improbable that they might, in time, become dissatisfied, if they were allowed less latitude or less freedom of action than their Irish brethren."

"Well, there is doubtless a great deal in what you say," General Montague remarked, "but Ireland is not the only country under British rule that is dissatisfied with present arrangements. I know there is a growing feeling of discontent in Canada which, sooner or later, will end in open rupture unless your government's policy of thrusting a British representative on them every five years, to fill the position of governor-general, ceases. They object to paying out $50,000 salary, and as much more for expenses, to what some of them term a foreigner, and besides they would rather do their own selecting from among their own people."

"Is that really the case?" Lord Grandwell asked. "I haven't heard any complaints of that nature from the Canadians who visit our side. If such a feeling exists, why don't they make a protest, or sign a petition to the head government? If such a request were properly made by a sufficient number of citizens, I am quite sure it would be readily acceded to."

"I don't believe that makes so much difference," Tremaine remarked. "As a matter of fact there are quite a number of the best people in Canada (in the minority perhaps) who are delighted to have a representative of the English nobility among them. They would prefer, of course, some one of royal caste, and for my part, I have often wondered why the governor-generalships of the important English colonies have not been filled by appointments from the sovereign family, which receives about $3,150,000 per annum from the public crib, and for which little or no value is given in return, outside of the services rendered by the queen."

"They doubtless would fill the positions very satisfactorily," Lord Grandwell drily replied, "but the English people would rather keep them at home, and are perfectly willing to allow the sum you named for their maintenance, which"—laughing—"is very moderate indeed. Why, the Prince of Wales' family has only an annual allowance of

£86,000. That certainly is a very trifling sum to keep up appearances in a manner befitting the future king of Great Britain."

"The president of the United States only receives a salary of $50,000 per annum," Caldwell quietly observed.

"Yes, I know," answered the earl. "His dignified position—the highest in the land—is put on a parity with a simple bank or railroad president, and when he retires from office he is obliged to resume his former calling, or go into the business of raising chickens, as one of your former presidents is reported to have done. We consider that our royal family is paid very moderately indeed. Why the Emperor of Austro-Hungary receives an annuity of £775,000—which is £145,000 more than the queen's entire family gets, and even the Italian family receives as much as the latter—notwithstanding the impoverished condition of Italy; while the King of Prussia is allowed £775,000, besides the income from a vast amount of property out of which expenditures for court and royal family are paid. But if you think your presidents are well paid you should ascertain what the Czar of Russia's pittance amounts to annually. It is stated that he has an income of 24,000,000 roubles—the equivalent of which in English money would be something like £2,400,000—which is derived from estates of fully one million square miles, consisting of cultivated lands and forests, besides very valuable gold, silver, and other mines in Siberia. The czar, being absolute monarch of all he surveys, looks upon everything of that kind as private property, and accordingly pockets the income derived therefrom, while his subjects half the time are on the verge of starvation. So you see, Mr. Caldwell, your president is a very cheap man, especially as he is obliged to perform more hard work than all the queens and emperors put together."

"It is wonderful with what fortitude the people in the old world bear such heavy burdens," Arthur responded.

"I prophesy that before a great many years elapse, nearly all the European nations will be under the same form of government as the United States. Some day Italy and Spain will both have to be reorganized, because their treasuries are almost depleted and their credit is becoming exhausted; while Germany's present emperor seems to be doing all he can to goad his people into open rebellion by his dogmatic utterances, and I am inclined to think he will succeed, if he lives long enough. Great Britain will be one of the first to peacefully fall into line, because her people are among the most intelligent"—bowing to Lady Constance—"on the face of the earth. Canada is already restless, and desirous of throwing off the shackles. I have been told by people in a position to judge, that fully three-fourths of her population are in favor of independence, or annexation to the United States. There seems to be three political parties at present in Canada. The Colonial party, which wishes their country to remain as an English colony; the Annexation party, which favors a union with the United States, and the Independents, who wish to go it alone; and in the latter class may be found most of the Liberals. The Canadian people are peaceful and intelligent, and will, therefore, endeavor to secure their independence from England by constitutional rather than revolutionary means, and I am inclined to think England will not stand in the way of separation, when she becomes convinced that a large majority wish it. Her experience with the United States is still fresh enough in her memory to prevent such a suicidal policy as Lord North pursued. Don't you agree with me, Lord Grandwell?"

"I, of course, cannot state positively what my country would do in such an emergency," replied the earl, " but I do not think Canada will have to fight for her independence, unless"—laughing—" she gets into a squabble sometime with the States. Disraeli, Russell, Salisbury and Gladstone are all on record as favoring dissolution whenever Canada demands it, and I am willing to vote that way at the proper time. As far as I am concerned, it will make no difference to me whether Canada desires to sever her present ties for the purpose of establishing an independent government, or with the idea of becoming annexed to the United States, although I feel convinced that Parliament would not favor the latter plan. If our present relations with Canada are to be severed I believe that a state of absolute independence would be more beneficial to her than annexation, as she would not be hampered by any laws of the United States, and would therefore be in a position to offer any inducement she saw fit to newcomers. The Dominion ought to be an extremely prosperous country, blessed as it is with all the natural sources of wealth that have made the United States so rich and prosperous. I must confess it is a matter of wonder to me when I look at the growth of the latter country during the last seventy years, and compare it with Canada's. In one case the progress made is simply marvelous, while in the other the lack of growth amounts almost to a standstill—if you place the statistics of the two countries side by side. Canada is the older country of the two, by almost one hundred years, with an area as large as the United States and possessing nearly all the same physical advantages that the latter does. Compare the population of these two countries: one has 72,000,000 people while the other has less than 5,000,000, or about the same as Ireland or Scotland: yet the North American countries are located side by side, with nothing but a latitudinal line dividing them, and both apparently offering equal advantages to settlers. It is one of the mysteries, and can only be accounted for by the fact that Canada is a few degrees farther north. That at least is the interpretation I would put on it."

"Permit me to differ with you, Grandwell," M. Rémiere said. "The study you have made of the internal workings of each country should have enabled you to form a more correct opinion than the one you have given. The United States has forged ahead so rapidly of, not only Canada, but every other country as well, for the reason that her shores offer an asylum to the poor, friendless creatures who are driven from their native hearths by laws so oppressive that they are really a burden, and in the end become unbearable. It is quite natural, therefore, that these poor souls should turn their eyes in the direction of the great American Republic, where a hearty welcome is extended to all deserving persons, of whatsoever creed or nationality. Canada offers every encouragement to immigrants to settle on her broad domain, and doubtless could make them just as prosperous and happy as the States, but the fact that she is a colony of Great Britain is of itself sufficient to deter would-be settlers from invading her lands. They naturally wish to become citizens of a free and independent country, where the taxes they pay will not be used in keeping up large standing armies, ready for bloody wars—such as is done in their native countries, and where they are likely to be engrafted into service at any moment. It is this feeling which militates against Canada, and as long as she remains under British rule, her populative and industrial growth will be retarded—in fact, I may say, there will be no growth, except in the way of natural increase in the families already located there."

"You may be right," Lord Grandwell answered. "It is my intention to spend a few weeks in Canada, with a view of studying the question more closely. Parliament may be called upon soon to act in the matter, and I should like to be better posted than I am at present. General, supposing a majority of the Canadian people should prefer annexation to the United States to independence, do you think your countrymen would be eager for the alliance, and willing to assume the Dominion's outstanding obligations?"

"My country, I believe, would be willing to annex Canada," the General answered, "if her people were to make a formal request to us, and England interposed no objection. But there is no anxiety on our part to bring about the alliance. You must understand that we have sufficient territory to take care of ten times our present population and then not be overcrowded. In fifty years from now when our census shows a population of 175,000,000 people—as it most likely will by that time—we shall think about adding to our possessions. In the meantime, we are not showing any undue haste. The public debt of Canada figures for less than $300,000,000, consequently the United States would have no hesitation in assuming or guaranteeing it. Speaking in the Dominion's own interest, I should say that annexation would be the very best thing that could happen. It would not only give her a much larger population—owing to the dividing line between the two countries being obliterated—but it would build her up commercially. Our capitalists have built 180,000 miles of railroads in the United States, and would doubtless extend their operations into Canada, if she were flying the stars and stripes. Our large trunk lines would, instead of using the Grand Trunk or Canadian Pacific tracks, build their own branches to Montreal, Quebec, Toronto, Hamilton, Ottawa, and other principal places, which, of course, would have a tendency to make trade more active throughout the Dominion, especially as the custom duties would be entirely done away with. Nearly all of Canada's export trade is with the United States and Great Britain—about one-third with the former and two-thirds with the latter. Now, with a suspension of duties, you can readily see what an advantage the Canadian merchants would gain. They produce yearly $12,000,000 worth of cheese, nearly all of which has to be sold abroad—that is to say, 3,000 miles away—whereas a great part of it could be disposed of in New York state alone, and at much better figures, but for the custom duty now in force. The same thing applies to hay, barley and other products from

Canadian soil which they can now sell to greater advantage in Europe, owing to the prohibitory taxes imposed in the United States. So you see, earl, Canada would be much benefited if she were allied to the United States."

"I must admit, General, from your showing, that such would appear to be the case. But would it not be the reverse with your country? Knock off your duties and you put Canadian products on the same footing with your own."

"It would appear so from the first glance," General Montague replied. "You must take into consideration, however, that our exports to Canada are quite large—fully $20,000,000 in excess of our imports—so that closer trade relations would in all probability be of equal benefit to us, by increasing our shipments across the border. You may rest assured the United States Government would be careful to see that the Dominion States traded with the other states in the Union to the fullest possible extent. There would be no trouble on that score. In other ways the alliance would be of greater advantage to the Canadas. Money would be sent from our side to start new industrial enterprises, and immigration would flow in streams that way. Instead of the United States drawing one hundred thousand settlers annually from Canada, she would entice double that number from us, besides droves from the old world. You must realize that the marvelous growth of our country is due in a large measure to the number of foreigners who settle on our shores—averaging, I believe, fully five hundred thousand persons each year. That is what Canada needs badly, but until she breaks loose from England her wishes in this respect are not likely to be gratified. So take my advice, Lady Constance, and do a little missionary work for Canada amongst your friends when you return home. Dismemberment means practically nothing to England, but very much to her colony."

"I will see what can be done when I return home," she laughingly answered. "I am afraid, however, that the first move will have to come from the Canadians themselves. Thus far they have done nothing in that direction, other than to publish newspaper articles now and then, which, unhappily for the cause, are not seen by the controlling spirits at home; or if they are, little interest is attached to them, owing to the general belief in England that Canada is quite contented to remain as she is. But don't you think we have talked politics long enough? The tables have long since been cleared off, and we need fresh air. Besides, I know these men are longing for their cigars. The conversation must have been highly interesting, otherwise they would not have foregone that pleasure so long."

" I agree with you, Lady Constance, in all things," Arthur remarked. " I am inclined to think, however, that a small portion of out-of-doors will satisfy your wants this evening, as it is quite chilly on deck, and you will have to be a peripatetic if you wish to keep warm. As I have always been one "—he added—" I shall be most happy to take a stroll, if you will permit me to accompany you."

"Thanks, Mr. Caldwell, I shall be glad to have you," Lady Constance replied.

Miss Montague accepted a similar invitation from the earl—much to Tremaine's disappointment,—as he had been anticipating such a pleasure for himself. He was obliged, therefore, to be contented with her uncle's company, and M. Rémiere (Mrs. Montgomery being indisposed) making up his mind that he would have to be more wide-awake in the future, if he wished to forestall the earl.

CHAPTER VIII.

"THE salon has rather a deserted appearance this morning, Miss Montague. I am afraid last night's blow was too much for the ordinary passenger to stand. Have you heard how it has fared with our friends?"

The speaker was Mr. Tremaine—the only one of the party besides Miss Montague—who had put in an appearance at the breakfast table. There was really a good excuse, however, for their non-attendance, as the seas had cut up pretty rough during the night—in fact there had been what the captain called a regular old-fashioned blow.

"Yes, I stopped at Lady Constance's and Mrs. Montgomery's rooms," answered Miss Montague, "and although they are not exactly ill, they felt a trifle upset, and preferred to remain in their rooms. My uncle sent me word that he would remain invisible until the ship's motion was more to his liking, and the steward brought word from Lord Grandwell and M. Rémicre that they would not breakfast with us this morning, but hoped to show themselves later. It would seem, therefore, as though you and I were the only ones to answer the roll call. To be quite candid with you, it required an exertion on my part to get here, and if I had not made a compact with you and Mr. Caldwell to be on hand each meal, I might have been tempted to do as the others have done. What has become of him? He surely is not going to play the invalid, after entering into an agreement with us to occupy his place each meal?"

"No," Tremaine answered, "Arthur is all right, but he always requires a few hours more sleep than others. He will doubtless turn up before long. What are you going to do with yourself all day? I am afraid it is not over-pleasant on deck, although the wind seems to be moderating."

"I have several things to do," Miss Montague replied. "I expect to read a chapter or two from 'Ben Hur,' in which I am greatly interested, talk a little with some agreeable person who will kindly lend me his ear and answer any questions I may put to him, and if this rocking motion subsides sufficiently to permit of it, I expect to take my customary walk on deck, provided I can get some one to accompany me."

"In all of which I am at your service," Fred said, "to say nothing of the pleasure it will afford me to attend you. I would suggest, however, that you dispense with 'Ben Hur' for to-day. It is a most delightful book, and one which I read with the greatest of pleasure. I am afraid, however, if you get started you will become so interested that you will be loath to lay it aside to indulge in ordinary conversation with me."

"Very well, Mr. Tremaine, I promise not to read until you get tired of talking to me. Will that do? If the others don't turn up, you may have to look after me during the whole day. In that case you are likely to be overtaxed."

"I am not heartless enough," Tremaine replied, "no matter how tempting the prospect seems, to wish our friends a whole day's illness; but at the same time, I cannot help saying, that if they prefer to remain in their staterooms, I shall not complain on account of being left alone with you, but on the other hand, shall consider myself twice blessed."

"Very well, I will take you at your word. If you have finished your breakfast let us go on deck and see what the weather prospects are."

On reaching the deck they found that with every lunge the boat made, large quantities of water were shipped, wetting the decks from stem to stern, consequently there was no alternative but to remain indoors for the present. Acting on Miss Montague's suggestion, they made their way to the music-room which they found nearly empty—not over half-a-dozen people being in there.

"Judging by the depopulated appearance of this shell," Tremaine remarked, "I should imagine that last night's blow amounted almost to a hurricane, and I am wondering how you and I are able to be up and about while nearly every one else seems to have surrendered without a struggle."

"It does seem strange, does it not?" said Miss Montague. "I suppose a determination to be out at all hazards had something to do with it, and I am glad that I made the effort. Before settling down to your all day's task, I would like to have you run down, if you don't mind, to Uncle Charles' stateroom and ascertain if anything can be done for his comfort."

Fred, of course, readily acquiesced, and shortly afterward returned with the report that General Montague was resting fairly comfortable, and asked for nothing further than a return of the seas to their normal condition.

"I promised him that," Fred laughingly said, "and received his grateful thanks. He fairly beamed when I informed him how few of the passengers had made their appearance—remarking that misery liked company, and that a person should always be satisfied to train with the majority."

"Yes, uncle is a good philosopher, and a firm believer in the adage that 'what can't be cured must be endured.' If we could all accept the trials and tribulations which beset us in that spirit, how much lighter life's weary burdens would seem."

"I agree with you," Tremaine answered, "but you must recollect that we are not all constituted alike. How is it though, that you speak of life's cares in such a grave tone? I cannot believe that you have much to worry about, but on the other hand should imagine that you managed to grasp the world's best pleasures."

"I am like every one else, Mr. Tremaine, in that respect. Sometimes in gathering flowers, you know, we unexpectedly run across a prickly thorn. I remember nearly four years ago, my father crossed the ocean with me for the purpose of placing me in school. It was my wish to finish my education abroad, and I anticipated so much pleasure in doing it. Yet in a few months' time poor papa was taken away, and even the consolation of being with him during his last hours was denied me, as he died so suddenly, there was no chance for me to reach his bedside."

A tear rolled down her cheek as she said this and her last words ended in a sigh, showing plainly the deep attachment she must have felt for her father and the sorrow his death had occasioned.

"Your experience was indeed a very sad one," Fred said in a sympathetic voice. "Pray excuse me for being the innocent cause of recalling your sorrow, which I know must have cut in deeply and which years alone can efface. We unwittingly drop a remark sometimes, without realizing that it may awake memories which are better left unrecalled."

"You need not reproach yourself, Mr. Tremaine, for anything you have said. I seldom allow my feelings to get the better of me, but the disagreeable weather and the desolate appearance of the vessel this morning has doubtless made me a little nervous. The rolling and plunging of the boat all night made sleep next to impossible, and when I am deprived of that, I get up feeling unlike my natural self. However, I did not bring you in here to talk about my woes or myself, but," smiling, "relied upon you to introduce an enlivening subject for conversation."

"Leaving your woes in the background, Miss Montague, the subject otherwise is interesting—more so to me than any other we could hit upon. Tell me about your stay in Europe. Did you like it there?"

"Very much indeed. The first two years were spent in study and the balance in travel and sight-seeing. Lady Carleton, the wife of one of uncle Charles' English partners, took me under her care, and for nearly two years we have been inseparable—spending a portion of our time in one country, until we got tired of it and then visiting another—and so on until we had finally seen everything we cared to see. Lady Carleton has been so kind to me—if she had been my own mother she could not have done more. You know we have a business house in Paris also; consequently I was well looked after there by uncle's partners and their wives—in fact wherever I traveled I met some one who seemed to be connected in a business way with us. You will understand, therefore, that everything was done to make my life a happy one and on the whole I was contented, although I longed at times to be in my own country."

"Why did you stay away so long?" Fred asked.

"Uncle Charles, who is my guardian, thought I had better see as much of European life as possible before returning home, and he was also anxious that I should become proficient in the French, German and Italian languages."

"All of which you accomplished, I suppose."

"Yes," laughing, "and to please uncle I also learned to speak Spanish."

"So that you are a regular walking-school of languages," Fred laughingly said. "Did you study anything else?"

"Oh, yes, lots of things. My real object, however, in going to Europe, was to have my voice properly trained and to study instrumental music."

"There is no need of my asking if you succeeded in that also, as with you it is *fait accompli* before you have commenced."

"I am afraid, Mr. Tremaine, you flatter me. But relative to music: I succeeded fairly well, at least I have been told so by eminent masters. You shall judge, however, for yourself when you pay me a call at my home in New York."

"I am exceedingly obliged for your invitation to call, and hope to avail myself of it when we return. I trust, however, you will not deny me until then the privilige of hearing you sing. You know"—laughing—"music-rooms," glancing at the piano, "are rather suggestive places when a prima donna is around."

"I hope you will not be disappointed when you hear me," Miss Montague answered, "which will probably be in New York, as I never sing in public places of this kind."

"Very well, I must be contented to wait until we land on Manhattan Island. Would that it were to-day, I don't mean that," hastily correcting himself. "I shall be glad to hear you sing, but in the meantime—you must forgive me for saying it—I am willing to postpone that delightful event for a week or ten days provided it will prolong our sea trip, and you will permit me to bask in the sunshine of your presence."

"That would imply illness to the other passengers, Mr. Tremaine, for ten whole days. As my uncle is one of them, I naturally object on humanitarian grounds"—smiling mischievously—"if upon no other."

Evidently wishing to turn the conversation, she said, "I have given you an account of my life abroad and shown you in part what I have accomplished: now I want to know if you think I am capable of learning the intricacies of finance. You remarked a little while ago that it was *fait accompli* when I commenced a thing. Do you think it would apply to the study of finance, if I were to take that branch up in earnest?"

"I have no doubt you would excel in that line, as in anything else," Fred replied. "Although it is such an extensive subject it would naturally require a great deal of study to become in any degree proficient. In fact it would take a lifetime to master all the different branches of finance—its scope is such a wide one—and even then you would find something to learn, as with the evolution of the world some new point is brought to light each day. I take it for granted, however, that you don't wish to go into the subject so deeply as that. Tell me what you wish to know and perhaps I can enlighten or help you."

Hesitating a moment Miss Montague finally said, " I may as well take you into my confidence, although I have never even broached the subject to my uncle "— Pausing for a moment again, as though debating where to begin she continued, " Perhaps you are aware that I was the only child my father had and that his estate in consequence descended to me. What it consisted of, I am unable to state for the reason that my uncle, up to the present time, has had entire charge of it, although I know, of course, that it is extensive. I have the utmost confidence in Uncle Charles, and shall always be guided more or less by his advice, still I feel that papa would have liked me to become familiar with his property—in fact once in talking over this matter together, he gave me explicit instructions on that point. But beyond that I am naturally interested for my own sake, and I intend taking entire charge of my affairs as soon as I am competent to do so."

" Your resolution is to be highly commended," Fred said, " especially as the undertaking is a formidable one. Young ladies can learn to speak foreign languages fluently and become conversant in a short time with other things equally difficult, but when it comes down to matters of business, where figures play an important part, and good judgment is required, their pretty heads get confused, and they are forced to become dependent on others for help; all of which would seem to indicate that your sex is fitted for everything except business."

" I cannot agree with you altogether, Mr. Tremaine. You doubtless base your conclusions on a few unfortunate cases which have been indelibly stamped on your memory, where the persons you have been brought in contact with have shown more or less stupidity, owing, of course, to their lack of familiarity with the business in hand and the details connected with it. If they had received the same business training that a man does, don't you think they would be quite competent to take charge of their own affairs? I admit that the average woman displays a woeful amount of ignorance where business is concerned; but that could easily be remedied if she would devote a portion of her time to the study of it. Now that is what I propose doing, and as I cannot very well serve an apprenticeship in uncle's office, I must manage to get my schooling in some other way. The question, however, is, what is the best mode of learning, and at what point am I to start?"

As she expounded her ideas, clothed in clear and convincing language, and at the same time expressed in face and manner such a determination to succeed, Tremaine thought to himself, "No wonder her father amassed a large fortune, if he was fortified with the same kind of spirit with which his daughter is endowed."

Aloud he said, "There is no question, Miss Montague, of your succeeding in anything you undertake; because when you attempt to do a thing you make it the paramount object, and stick to it until you have mastered the details. The majority of your sex are lacking in that respect; they start in all right, but unfortunately after a first attempt, if the object proves difficult of attainment, they are apt to abandon it, and allow some one to act for them. In proof of this, how many women do you suppose manage their own estates?"

"Why a very large number, I suppose."

"Your supposition, then, is a wrong one. They constitute a very small minority where the estate is of any size; and not only that, they know so little about their own business affairs, their agents can cheat and hoodwink them in the most flagrant manner, without fear of detection."

"Is there not all the more reason then, why I should become familiar with my affairs? There is no one in the whole world I would sooner trust than Uncle Charles, but in all probability I shall outlive him by a score or two of years, in which event it is quite essential that I should be prepared to act for myself."

"I agree with you perfectly, Miss Montague, and I am sure your resolution will commend itself to your uncle. I am quite free to confess, however, that very few young ladies would care to undertake such an immense task as yours will be. You, of course, don't realize it, but it will take a great deal of your time and attention, and leave very little leisure for social duties,—so dear to the hearts of most women occupying your position."

"Oh! I realize that it will not be an easy thing, and that I have a great deal to learn; but as for the pomps and gaieties of society, I can surely afford to forego some of them, although I do not intend to drop out of the social world entirely. I shall endeavor to fill my social obligations satisfactorily, and in addition devote sufficient time to properly look after my estate. Our talk has taken quite a business turn, has it not, Mr. Tremaine?" laughing heartily as she realized the scope of their conversation. "One would think that you were my business adviser, to hear the way I have been confiding to you my future plans and ambitions;" and again she indulged in laughter, which provoked similar strains from Fred.

As soon as their merriment had subsided, the latter said, "I look upon it as a matter of confidence that you have talked so freely to me of your affairs, and I shall be only too glad to give you any advice in my power—although, of course, General Montague is better fitted in every way to tell you all that is needful to carry out your plans. As I said before, you will find enough to keep you busy; and although I had my doubts at first about your being able to discharge the onerous duties you will be called upon to perform, I am quite convinced, after hearing your lucid ideas on the subject, that you are well qualified to undertake the task."

"I prize your opinion, coming from a business man, very much, Mr. Tremaine. Do you know that is what I have been trying to draw out of you ever so long; but for some preverse reason you have been very chary of your praise."

"I considered it my duty," Fred replied, "to put both sides of the question plainly before you—as a physician did to me once, when I sought his advice in reference to becoming a member of his profession. You have passed through the ordeal though better than I did, because I backed out when he related to me the hardships of an M. D., whereas you are more determined than ever to go ahead."

"Yes, because I know I am right. That you were right in not taking up the medical profession is also proven by your success as a financier."

"How do you know I am a success?" Fred asked.

Miss Montague hesitated slightly before replying, and then smilingly said, "Your friend, Mr. Caldwell, has told me of your wonderful achievements in the financial world. He has given such glowing accounts of you, I have quite made up my mind to add your name to my list of bankers."

"I am exceedingly obliged to you," Fred replied, "and shall be delighted to enroll such a fair client on my books. It is proper to state, however, that Arthur is slightly prejudiced in my favor; you must recollect that we are close friends, and make allowance accordingly."

"A phrenologist once told me," Miss Montague retorted, "that I was a good reader of human nature, and would rarely be deceived; you must permit me, therefore, to make my own selections."

"O! I am not going to interpose an objection; clients are too hard to secure for that. But when do you propose starting in on your business training?"

"I have already started in to learn. I should have thought that your perspicacity would have disclosed to you the object of my questioning. I mean to talk finance with every well-informed person I meet hereafter, and read everything I can find, having a bearing on the subject, until I become thoroughly posted. As my banker, I naturally expect you to help me all you can; tell me what to study and how to go about it. When I talk on business topics, I feel as ignorant as a young child just starting in at school, and no doubt I appear so."

"It is not to be expected that you should know much about a line of study you have never taken up," Fred said; "but where darkness now exists light will soon penetrate, and in time you will be as conversant with matters of business as you are with foreign languages. As your father's estate doubtless consists principally of stocks, bonds, mortgages and realty, it seems to me that it is necessary for you to become familiar with everything relating to them. For instance, you will have to study the railroads of the United States, so as to determine which of them offer the safest and best securities for investment. Your uncle, of course, could advise you as to that, but that would not be acting on your own judgment, as you propose doing. Then again you will have to get posted on realty in New York city, so that you can determine what are bargains and what are not. When you have reached thus far, you will be in a position to make judicious investments—to separate the wheat from the chaff—and that I take it is the most essential thing for you to learn. You must not go in with the idea of making money, but rather to keep what you have got. The natural accumulation of interest from your present holdings, if safely invested, will increase your principal sufficiently without the necessity of jeopardizing any part of it in speculation. When securities are selling high enough to warrant a decline, or surrounding conditions are such that a fall in values seems imminent, it will, of course, be advantageous for you to dispose of some of your holdings with a view of repurchasing at a lower level. In order to accomplish this, it will be necessary for you to keep a large portion of your funds invested in marketable securities, such as are dealt in on the New York Stock Exchange. In handling a large estate like yours, it is absolutely necessary that you should become as well posted on the different classes of securities as possible; keep pace of the railroads you are interested in; ascertain if they are conservatively and well managed, and watch their earnings. Fight shy of a railroad that has a large floating debt, or is in danger of accumulating one, because, sooner or later, such indebtedness causes the borrower trouble. Another thing to keep pace of, is the increased mileage of a railroad. A great many companies which should be self-sustaining now, became bankrupt, owing to the building of extensions in barren territory or through localities already occupied by other lines. In either case, such policy is generally suicidal, because the roads cannot possibly earn the fixed charges on their new branches for years to come, and the losses thus entailed fall upon the stockholders, resulting in diminished dividends or a stoppage of them altogether. Is my meaning clear, Miss Montague? if not, don't hesitate to ask any questions you see fit."

"Perfectly clear. You are well versed in didactics, and I am extremely obliged to you for your enlightening me. I am beginning to understand what is expected of me, and with a few more lessons such as you have just given, shall imagine myself more or less of a financier—more than I was, but less than I hope eventually to be. You have given me a good text to study, and I shall endeavor to profit by it."

"Very well then!" he said. "Thus endeth the first lesson."

"Are there no books or papers published," she inquired, as though loath to leave the subject, "which will give me an insight into railroad affairs?"

"Oh, yes," he replied. I can furnish you with plenty of that kind of literature. The brokers' bible, I imagine, will keep you busy for some months to come."

"What is the brokers' bible?" she smilingly asked.

"A large book called 'Poor's Manual of Railroads,'" he answered, "which is published yearly. It contains full and accurate information of all the railroads in the United States; and in every banker's and broker's office a copy of it can be found. When you pick up your newspaper, instead of selecting the society column for information, you must read carefully the market reports which are published daily. You will thus become familiar with financial matters, and at the same time enable yourself to keep abreast of the financial times. If you faithfully follow the programme I have laid out, you will have little time for novel reading for several months. Now if you have no objection, I propose we go on deck; I think we can do so with safety."

CHAPTER IX.

A few moments afterward, Tremaine and his fair companion were on the deck indulging in a "go as you please walk," or more accurately describing it, "go as they did not *please*," for the ship's irregular action made their footsteps uncertain, and instead of walking a horizontal line, they found themselves one minute brushing the side of the cabin, and the next in close proximity to the guard-rail. Fred, however, found no fault with the situation, especially as he occasionally got a pleasant bump from his companion, and although it occurred to her several times that it was a case of walking under difficulties, she uttered no protest, and on the whole rather enjoyed it. Connected talk, however, was out of the question, and with the exception of a word now and then, little was said on either side. Miss Montague was mentally taking stock of what Mr. Tremaine had been telling her of finance. She had no misgivings as to her being able to fill the rôle she had laid out for herself, and was so fascinated with the idea, she was longing to return to the subject and receive a second lesson. She restrained from doing so, however, partly because it was impossible to carry on a jointed conversation, and also to a feeling that perhaps her companion was not interested in her affairs sufficiently to warrant a resumption of the subject right away. It may seem strange to the reader that a young lady occupying Miss Montague's position should care to assume such responsibilities as she proposed undertaking, and I myself have wondered how the notion first entered her head; the only plausible reason being that she inherited the taste for finance from her father and uncle. Be that as it may, she had fully determined to become her own agent in managing her estate, and as she possessed the necessary qualifications to do so, no one who knew her, could doubt that she would prove a success. Some such thoughts as these were passing through Tremaine's mind as he walked by her side, and something connected therewith caused him to suddenly laugh. Miss Montague caught the sound and enquired the reason.

"I was wondering to myself," Fred said, "if, when you learn the ways of Wall street, you will ever ' squeeze ' any of your friends on the Exchange."

"I don't think I quite catch your meaning," she answered, with some show of surprise at his question.

"Pardon me for indulging in ' street ' talk," he hastily said. "I meant if you would ever corner a stock on the Exchange and squeeze some of the persons who were ' short ' of it."

"You will have to first enlighten me as to the meaning of ' short,' " she smilingly answered. "You must recollect that you are talking to a neophyte."

"No he isn't, Miss Montague, but rather to a nymph," they heard somebody say.

Looking around they saw that the remark emanated from Mr. Caldwell, who had come up behind, and had caught the last part of Miss Montague's sentence.

"How do you do, Mr. Caldwell;" "Hello, Arthur, where have you been all the morning?" came from the other two, simultaneously.

"Where have I been?" that gentleman remarked. "You should rather tell me where you have been. Lord Grandwell, M. Rémiere and I have been on a still hunt for you all morning, and not meeting with success we have been endeavoring to kill time in a game of cards."

"At which I suppose *you* were successful," Tremaine smilingly remarked, with the accent on you.

"Yes," Arthur laughed. "I am afraid I understood the game slightly better than the others. However, they are not much out and I have promised to give them satisfaction before we reach New York. They are fascinated with the great American game, and the earl declares that it beats baccarat."

"You ought not to play cards for money," Miss Montague said; "you should leave that to professional gamblers."

"What! and let them have all the fun?" Arthur exclaimed. "That would certainly be an act of magnanimity. You don't mean to say you have never been to Monte Carlo?"

"Yes, I have been there," Miss Montague answered, "but not to indulge in any game of chance."

"You surprise me," Arthur said. "Fred and I went there for a day, and staid nearly a week. The last night we were there, I very nearly broke the bank, and am quite positive I should have done so if this man," indicating Tremaine, "had not begged me to quit. It was an opportunity of a lifetime, and I shall never have such a chance to legitimately break a bank again. Everything ran my way and all the inmates of the room were crowded around my table in the greatest state of excitement. Fred, you were a mean fellow that night; I know I could have broken the bank. But were they not mad when I left the building with my pockets stuffed full of their money?" and Caldwell laughed heartily at the recollection.

"You were certainly very lucky," Tremaine said, "but the chances are that you would have been a loser in the end if you had remained much longer. Why, Miss Montague, you never saw such a reckless person in your life. With every new deal he was increasing his bets—five, ten, and fifteen thousand, and I expected every minute to see him put his whole fortune on the table."

"I couldn't do that," Arthur laughed, "because the most of it was tied up in New York. Besides, you must give me credit for being the coolest man in the room. You also ought to have remembered that I am a speculator by profession, and to have made due allowances accordingly."

"I am afraid you are incorrigible, Mr. Caldwell," Miss Montague remarked. "The Stock Exchange must be a dreadful place for one's morals. Do you go in for speculation to the extent that this man does, Mr. Tremaine?"

"No, Miss Montague, I do not," he said; and laughingly added, "but perhaps it is due to the fact that I am not blessed with an independent fortune like Arthur. I have not accumulated sufficient yet to hazard the attempt at breaking the bank of Monte Carlo. If I had been left a fortune perhaps I might be more courageous."

"You are better without it," she replied, "if you would use it in such a fashion."

"Wealth is a snare," quoth Arthur. "I once attended a lecture given by a prominent person in New York. Looking right at me he said: 'There are some sons to whom the inheritance of their father's wealth was a damning curse.' I felt uncomfortable for a minute or two, and was on the point of asking the speaker to take my inheritance and enjoy himself for the remainder of his days, as he doubtless—from his standpoint—could make better use of it than I. Self-consideration, however, knocked out my benevolent desire, and I left the hall thinking what a narrow escape I had. But to return to your aspersion against the Stock Exchange, Miss Montague; as a member of that much maligned institution, I must correct the erroneous impression you seem to have formed concerning it. You are not, perhaps, aware that its members are comprised of some of the best church-going citizens of New York, a sample of which you find in the highly respectable Mr. Tremaine by your side, and your eminent uncle, whom I regret to say, is not here to speak for himself; and last—but by no means least—your humble servant," bowing low with mock seriousness, "who believes in these lines:

"'Give me good proofs of what you have alleged:
'Tis not enough to say—in such a bush
There lies a thief—in such a cave a beast.'"

"The Stock Exchange has an able defender in you, Mr. Caldwell," she answered. "But I have not made any allegations against your sacred Exchange. As you have quoted poetry it is permissible for me to return an answer in kind. I recall some lines from Mrs. Hale's pen, which seem to fit your case exactly:

> "'None have accused thee; 'tis thy conscience cries,
> The witness in the soul that never dies;
> Its accusation, like the moaning wind,
> Of wintry midnight, moves thy startled mind.'"

"Fred, my memory refuses to recall anything appropriate to answer this young lady. Kindly draw on your stock of knowledge to vindicate ourselves, otherwise she will think that her words have struck home."

Thus beseeched, Tremaine quoted from Heath, without a moment's hesitation,

> "'Good actions crown themselves with lasting days,
> Who deserves well needs not another's praise.'"

When he had finished, Caldwell exclaimed, triumphantly, "That's the thing, Fred; 'good actions speak louder than words'; there is no need of our saying anything else." Turning to Miss Montague, he said, "We accept your apology, and sometime when you are down on Wall street come in and see us, and we will present further proof of our uprightness. With the exception of a few ambidexter cusses—I beg your pardon I meant to say persons—there are no more honorable men to be found anywhere. But to change the subject; have you noticed, Miss Montague, that this craft is riding the sea more gently? We seem to be leaving the storm behind; and I should not wonder if we had a pleasant afternoon after all. By the way, I wonder what our day's run will be? I went into the auction pool yesterday, and as I hold the low number, should not be surprised if I won the stakes, as the rough weather must have retarded our progress considerably. Miss Montague, let me take a chance for you in the next pool. I guarantee success or money refunded. Lady Constance has authorized me to go in both the hat and auction pools for her, and I would like to be your agent also. Do you consent?"

"I don't think I know what they are," Miss Montague laughingly said. "Besides, I am afraid it is a sort of gambling, and you know I could not consistently go in for that kind of thing, after the talk we have just had on that subject."

"Oh, no! There is no gambling in this," Arthur said, decisively. "Have I not guaranteed you against loss? There is not even a shade of speculation about it, it is simply an investment—that is all;" and without waiting for her consent, he added, "I will get you a good number, never fear;" and hurried away, fearful lest she might decline the offer.

After he had gone, Miss Montague said, "Mr. Caldwell does not permit any chance to speculate to pass him by, does he?"

"No," Fred laughed. "He is a natural born speculator. Perhaps it can be accounted for by the fact that his ventures nearly always turn out profitably. His luck, shrewdness, sagacity or foresight, or whatever it may be called—and I am inclined to think it is a combination of all—is simply wonderful. If he goes 'long' or 'short' of the stock market he makes money on both sides where others seem to fail. It sounds incredulous, I know; but it is nevertheless the truth."

"You have used those expressions 'long' and 'short' again. Won't you please tell me what they mean?" she asked.

"That is easily done," he answered. "A person who buys stock to hold is said to go 'long' of it and one who sells stock which he does not possess, goes 'short' of it."

"But how can he sell that which he does not possess?"

she persisted, which brought forth a peal of laughter from Tremaine. "You ought not to laugh at my ignorance," she said. "Did they teach you those terms at school?"

"No, Miss Montague."

"How do you suppose then, that I am familiar with them? You know you promised to teach me."

"And so I will," he contritely answered. "Pardon me for laughing. The terms are so common, I thought every one understood them; but of course you have had no opportunity to become acquainted with our 'street' jargon. A person makes a 'short' sale—meaning something he does not own—because he believes the price will go lower, thereby enabling him to buy it back at a cheaper figure. Through the machinery of a broker's office he is permitted to do this —the broker furnishing the stock for delivery if he has it on hand, or if not, borrowing it from some fellow member. The 'bears' believe that stocks were made to sell, and the 'bulls,' of course, that they were made to buy and hold."

"I have heard the terms 'bulls' and 'bears' before," she said. "Tell me how they came to be applied to stock-dealing."

"I have been told," he replied, "that they were suggested by the bull and bear fights which used to be a fashionable sport many years ago in a place called Smithfield, just outside of London. When the bull happened to be the better fighter of the two, he tossed his antagonist *up*; whereas the bear endeavored to pull his adversary *down*. Thus the term 'bull' became applied to a speculator who worked for, or favored higher prices, and the word 'bear' to one who wished values to go lower."

Miss Montague listened to this explanation very attentively, and when Tremaine had finished, said, "What right has any person to depreciate the value of another's securities? It seems to me that such a process must work incalculable injury to the people who are, what you just now called 'long.' It certainly cannot be pleasant, to say the least, to a person who is the owner of a certain stock, to have the 'bears' depress the price of his security and otherwise injure it. That assuredly cannot be a fair or legal proceeding. Do you mean to say that if I own a dwelling house, any one can attack its value with impunity?"

"I am not trying to justify the tactics of the 'bears,'" Tremaine answered; "although it is considered perfectly legitimate on Wall street. If you want to sell your house you naturally use all the arguments at your command to talk it up in order to obtain a good price; whereas the purchaser picks all the flaws he can in your argument in an endeavor to get your property as cheaply as possible. You must remember that it takes two to make a bargain. On your side you look through a telescope so that it will magnify the value of your holdings, while the buyer, on the contrary, looks through the reverse end of the instrument so as to diminutize it as much as possible. But after all, it is the same with securities as anything else traded in. If the demand exceeds the supply, prices go up; while, on the other hand, if the amount offered is excessive, or more than the market will take, prices must inevitably seek a lower level; surrounding conditions generally regulate this, although there is seldom a dearth of securities in the American market, for the reason that the railroads in our country are of an aqueous quality, and are kept so constantly 'watered' by the artesian wells along the routes, that a fresh supply is always cropping out. So you see the 'bears' are sometimes justified in saying such and such a property is selling too high, and in exposing its weak character, although the 'bulls' do not think so. I have given you a few apagogical illustrations to show this, although I don't wish you to think that I espouse the 'bear' side or favor their methods of trading."

"Your arguments are always strong and convincing, and you have presented the matter to me in a new light," she replied; "still, I am not quite ready to believe that it is right for any one to wilfully depreciate the value of another person's property. I suppose, however, that a little practical experience on Wall street would do much to change my opinion in this respect."

"Very likely," he replied; and added, "a strange feature in connection with the Smithfield fights is, that they were finally stopped, not on account of the pain inflicted on the animals, but because of the pleasure it afforded the spectators. I presume if you had your way, you would suppress the Stock Exchange fights—not because of the pleasure it affords the 'bull' and 'bear' traders, but owing to the misery it causes the spectators—that is to say—the investors."

"Yes," she laughed; "and I think the authorities themselves ought to have suppressed the Stock Exchange fights rather than those at Smithfield."

"In that event," he answered, "there would be small use for an Exchange, and less use for commission brokers. As I unfortunately belong to the latter class, you cannot expect me to coincide with you. A speculator, in order to make money and be happy, should change from the 'bull' to 'bear' side, or vice versa, according to the surrounding conditions. If this method were adopted by the 'lambs' on entering Wall street there would be fewer 'lame ducks' floating around."

"Lambs and lame ducks," she exclaimed. "What have they got to do with Wall street?"

"A great deal," Fred smilingly answered. "The 'street' is full of them. A 'lamb' is a new beginner, who possesses some money but no experience; while a 'lame duck' is an 'ex-lamb,' shorn of his money, but not lacking in experience. Our 'street' vocabulary will become familiar to you in time. You are a 'lamb' as yet yourself, speaking in the vernacular, but you must endeavor to gain experience without becoming a 'lame duck.'"

Tremaine's explanation afforded much amusement to Miss Montague, and she echoed his wish concerning herself.

Presently Caldwell joined them again and triumphantly exclaimed: "I won the pool by a margin of nearly fifty miles. Your turn to-morrow, Miss Montague; remember I have guaranteed it. In the meantime you had better go down to luncheon—it is almost over with now. Wind Fred up, and he never knows when to stop talking," and he added, mischievously, "you two must have had a long day of it all by yourselves. I will be on hand to enliven you this afternoon. Come along, or Lord Grandwell will be instituting a search party. He has been on pins and needles all morning, and wondering if Miss Montague were ill." At which remark Miss Montague slightly colored but said nothing; while Tremaine looked daggers at his friend, evidently wishing that Arthur's thoughts would take another direction. In order to escape further raillery, they both hurried down to the salon, which proceeding was not lost on Arthur, and brought forth a rather forced smile from that gentleman.

CHAPTER X.

In the afternoon the elements—which had held a twelve hours' uninterrupted siege, thereby making the ocean fairly churn in their endeavors to show their procreative powers,—became amenable to reason, and our friends were once more able to sit on deck with comparative ease and comfort—General Montague, who still felt a little the worse for wear, being the only absent one.

Lord Grandwell's manner showed that he thought Miss Montague had been rather neglectful of him during the forenoon, in fact he said as much to her; but she gave little heed to his complaint—if such it could be called—other than to give a little good-natured laugh and to remind him that she was not responsible for the inebriate condition of the vessel, which made it necessary for him to keep to his stateroom.

His explanation that he was only a little later than usual in making his appearance, and that his efforts to find her were futile, simply brought forth a shake of her head, accompanied by an amused smile, which might imply that she received his statement with incredulity or, that it was a matter of inconsequence; he chose to put the former interpretation on it and would have continued to enquire more closely concerning her whereabouts, if she had not turned the subject by remarking to Lady Constance who was talking with Arthur about the "day's run"—

"Mr. Caldwell cannot fleece the 'lambs' on Wall street, consequently he is looking for victims here. Be careful how you put yourself in his clutches, Lady Constance, or you may become a 'lame duck,'" and she laughed gleefully at the look of mystification which overspread the other's features.

The terms had to be explained to Lady Constance and Arthur remarked —

"I see, Fred, you have been initiating this young lady;" and turning to her, added, "I don't think you will be an easy victim for any man," at which they all smiled, and something like the following occurred to each of the gentlemen present: "'Tis true, 'tis pity, and pity 'tis 'tis true."

Miss Montague all unconscious of the train of thought which had been aroused by Caldwell's jest, smiled more complacently than the rest, and said —

"It isn't nice, you know, to be victimized, Mr. Caldwell. I dislike the idea of being a poor little 'lamb' ready to be devoured by the first Wall street shark who happens along, and have therefore been taking lessons in finance; not, however, with any idea of entering your profession, I assure you"—laughing—"but simply as a matter of protection."

"That's right," Arthur observed. "The world is full of sharks, ready to gobble up the 'lambs,' but you will learn sometime that Wall street has no more in proportion than other trade-circles. My experience is that you find them in every channel of life, so your lessons in finance will do you no harm, whether you put them in practice or not. But there; I don't want to talk finance. I will leave that to Fred, who is an abler exponent of the subject than I. By the way, here are the pool numbers on to-morrow's run which I drew for you. I wish you could both win, but unfortunately there is only one prize and fifty chances. The whole numbers run from 426 to 475 inclusive. Your number is 470, Lady Constance, and a very good one, as we shall probably make fast time during the next twenty-four hours; we may as well bid it in, therefore, when the pools are auctioned off to-night. Your drawing, Miss Montague, in my estimation, is not worth much, being the smallest number in the set. As the lowest won to-day there will be a lively demand for your number to-night by people who won't take into consideration the fact that we are now making something like twenty knots an hour. I shall therefore let yours go at the sale and procure a higher one. What number do you want?"

"I must leave it to you," she replied, "inasmuch as you"—smiling mischievously—"possess the qualities of a speculum, which accurately reflects on your imagination, information in advance of others. Besides you know I told you I did not believe in speculation or any game of chance."

"Your argument is rather inconsistent, Miss Montague. Why do you call it a game of chance and at the same time liken my mind unto a reflector? If I possess penetration of the specular order, it seems to me that the element of risk is lacking and if that is eliminated then there is no chance to lose. However I do not claim those qualities; I simply weigh the evidence for or against a thing, and govern myself accordingly. I call it good judgment. Now common sense tells me that we are likely to have a good day's run, because everything favors it. I intend, therefore, if you approve, to bid for the highest number and you may take my word for it, it will be a gilt-edged investment and a big dividend payer. If all the securities on the Stock Exchange were half as safe, the 'bears' would have a hard time of it scrambling for a living;" and he chuckled to himself, as he thought of some of the inflated "footballs" on the "street," which were designated *investments*.

"There is no use in my trying to argue with you," Miss Montague said. "You are too well versed on the subject. If I were to say that playing cards for money was gambling, you would meet my statement with some argument tending to show that it was simply a gilt-edged investment."

"It might be under some circumstances," he laughed. "For instance, if you were playing with a greenhorn or stacked the cards. But there; I must not jest on the subject, otherwise you will think I am a *chevalier d' Industrie*. I acknowledge being a speculator, but nothing worse than that. If you will listen to me, some day I will try to prove to you by argument that the terms are not synonymous."

"As you are an interesting talker, Mr. Caldwell, on the subject of agiotage—and all others as well—I shall be only too glad to hear you"—Miss Montague rejoined—"and promise not to cavil at anything you may say—reserving the right, of course, to answer you in kind if you become a chaffinch"—she thought it best to add this, as she was not quite sure of her ground when talking with Arthur, who indulged sometimes in persiflage with such a serious manner, it was difficult to tell whether he was in jest or earnest.

He laughed good-naturedly at her remark, and promised to be "as solemn and earnest as a dominie delivering his Sunday sermon."

"If you assume that bearing," she replied, "I shall know you are jesting because it is not in you to be really serious. Besides, your *natural* manner"—smiling—"is not wholly disagreeable; only I like to know when I am listening to a person on a subject I am not familiar with, whether he is serious or not. I suppose I ought not to criticise a thing I know so little about, but it has always seemed to me that speculation tends to demoralize one's character."

"If that is so," Arthur replied, "then demoralization exists in nearly every walk of life, especially when applied to business, because no line of business is without it; even life itself is a speculation, for who can tell with absolute certainty what the morrow will bring forth; we may be living to-day and dead to-morrow; we run the risk of losing our lives in crossing the ocean or in riding on a railroad train, and consider it so hazardous we take out an accident policy. What is more speculative than a child's future? We spare no expense in fitting him for life's battles; and yet how often is it money thrown away? I admit that we do it partly from a sense of filial duty, but that does not alter the case in the least. If we knew that a boy would waste his days in riotous living, do you imagine that money would be spent in giving him a college education? No; we would rather apprentice him to a blacksmith at the age of sixteen. I contend, therefore,—leaving natural affection and all that it implies out of the question—that our main object in furnishing a boy with a liberal education, is to make him fit to earn his own livelihood. If he succeeds, the speculation is a good one—especially if he renders such assistance to his parents as may be necessary—but, on the other hand, if he fails"—here Arthur gave a shrug of the shoulders—" why the investment has been unprofitable, and the parents may be called upon to pay future assessments to keep their offspring out of the poorhouse."

"Your explanation is very clear, so far as it relates to life," Miss Montague observed, much amused. "Now let us hear to what extent speculation is allied to everyday business."

"There is no line of business without it," he replied, "from the manufacturer or wholesale dealer down to the peanut vender, the word *venture* enters into all their negotiations. Take, for instance, the former; he contracts for a large quantity of raw material, and keeps his wheels in motion—even when without orders—to turn out a big stock of goods so as to have them on hand ready to supply any possible demand. To do this he has probably been a borrower at his bank, expecting, of course, to pay the money back when his goods are sold. But suppose, for some reason or other, the usual demand does not materialize—as is frequently the case—the manufacturer finds himself loaded down with a large stock, and no money to take up his notes. The wholesale merchant is similarly situated; he is obliged to contract for supplies in advance of orders, trusting to luck or the ordinary demand to relieve him of them. Even should the season be a prosperous one, thereby enabling him to get rid of his goods, he is obliged, in most instances, to take his pay in notes, which may or may not be paid at maturity; for you must understand, ladies, that nine-tenths of the business transacted throughout the country is done on a system of credit. Is there any risk or speculation connected with this? The manufacturer and merchant will tell you there is, and an examination of their books will corroborate their statements. What I have said regarding the first handlers of goods, applies equally to the numerous retail merchants. Competition compels them to keep their shelves and counters well stocked at all seasons of the year, so as to meet any demand the public may make upon them; if the season proves an unprofitable one the goods have to be laid away until the fall or spring months come around again, by which time the styles most likely have undergone a change, thereby making them unsalable, excepting at a reduced cost. Under such circumstances, don't you think the merchant has been indulging in speculation just as much as a man who uses his money as margin in buying railroad stocks? For my part, I cannot distinguish much difference in the two operations."

"Perhaps not as far as the risk is concerned," Miss Montague interposed; "only one is a necessary business transaction and the other is not."

"Why not?" Arthur asked. "They both invest their money, according to their ideas, in something which they think will yield them better returns than could have been obtained if their funds had been deposited in a savings institution. I am not trying to prove that one investment is as safe as the other—that is a matter of judgment which does not enter into the question—I simply contend that speculation, or chance, enters into each operation. Does any one doubt this?"

As no one questioned his statement, Arthur took it for granted that his argument was unanswerable and continued—

"Take the farmers for instance; theirs is the most hazardous business known to man: they have all the elements to combat against in raising their crops; and from the time the seed is planted until the crops are finally harvested it is a period of doubt and uncertainty to them—not knowing whether the yield will be sparse or plentiful, and in utter ignorance as to the price they will eventually obtain for their products. Some of the larger farmers try to lessen this risk by selling options on the Exchanges against their growing crops, but there is risk in that also, because the yields may pan out less than anticipated, and in consequence they may find themselves 'short' of the market. Truly a farmer's life is not a happy one, and small wonder they are urging this and that wild scheme on Congress to alleviate their distress. But to give you another example of speculation, which is rather appropriate, seeing we are on a vessel: take the business of a shipbuilder—more particularly as it relates to government contracts—and what do we find? The owner stipulates to build a vessel within a stated time, on the lines of a certain model—which must show an acquired speed, of say—twenty knots an hour on her trial trip—under a penalty of forfeiting part of the agreed price if the boat does not meet all the requirements. He accepts these conditions, not knowing whether he will be able to fill them or not. Why? Because the government agrees to allow him a certain percentage, over and above the contract price, for any speed developed greater than that named. The cruiser New York, on her trial trip, averaged twenty-one knots an hour, which gave her builders an agio of $200,000 and speaks well for their knowledge of shipbuilding. The result, however, might have been different—in fact has been so in some instances, with other builders—in which case a penalty would have been exacted. Don't you all admit that there is as much speculation and risk attached to such a contract, as there would be in judicious buying of shares on the Stock Exchange?"

Again Arthur accepted silence as meaning consent, and continued, by apagogical examples, to prove that speculation entered into all kinds of business, and was therefore legitimate. He used arguments which the most of his hearers found unassailable, and which commanded the closest attention. Miss Montague did not raise captious or frivolous objections to any of his utterances, but now and then put in a word, more for the purpose of prolonging the discussion than for any other reason. The subject had a sort of fascination for her and she wanted to become as familiar with this branch of finance, and all others, as was possible. One thing is certain, she could not have found a person better posted on the subject than Caldwell; for what he did not know about speculation was hardly worth knowing. I have encountered a good many speculators in my time, but have rarely met one who was proficient to such a marked degree in self-reliance, good judgment, courage and prudence—all necessary factors in making a successful operator.

Arthur finally thought he had exhausted the topic—to his own, and everybody's satisfaction, but Miss Montague evidently still thirsted for knowledge, for she said—

"You have proven to us that speculation enters into all kinds of business but you have not shown that Stock Exchange speculations are legitimate, or even necessary."

"With you it's a case of being convinced against your will," he replied, "and I am afraid when I have finished you will be of the same opinion still. However "—laughing—" I don't intend to stop while there is any doubt in your mind as to my ability to explain every phase of the question. The Stock Exchange, you must know, was established for the purpose of facilitating the purchase and sale of corporate securities—primarily, stocks and bonds of railroads, although it is not confined to that class—as government, state, municipal and other kinds are traded in as well. The Exchange records the ruling prices of such securities as are dealt in, and these quotations are telegraphed to all parts of the country, thereby enabling the holders of similar securities, or would-be purchasers, banks and others to keep fully posted on the trend of values. Without an Exchange you will realize the difficulty buyers and sellers would have in coming together, and the ignorance each would be in, regarding market values. The want of such knowledge and facilities would necessarily work great hardships and engender fraud on the part of unscrupulous persons, who would not hesitate to give fictitious prices in buying and selling securities, whenever it could be done. Under existing arrangements—through a broker—you can invest in, or dispose of any securities listed on the Exchange, at the ruling quotations, which represent their market value. Without an Exchange it would be an utter impossibility to float the stock and bond issues of railroads, which practically implies that there would be no railroads built; you will understand therefore that the New York Stock Exchange has really been the means by which the United States have been developed to such a wonderful extent, for without the railroads, the vast area of the country would still be uninhabitated. So much for that part of it. I have told you that an outsider, through a commission broker, is always enabled to find a ready market for his securities at ruling quotations. I should have explained that this is made more easy, by reason of the fact that certain members on the floor of the Exchange—known as traders—stand ready, at all times, to take any security offered, or to sell any security wanted, at a given price—that is to say—at the bid and asked quotations. These traders are what you would designate speculators, and I am one of them. I buy this or sell that—not for the benefit of others, as you might infer from my explanation—but simply to make all I can out of it. Nevertheless my trading indirectly helps others by keeping the market alive. So you see, Miss Montague, while you would hardly class me as a philanthropist "—laughing— "you must admit that I am of some use to mankind."

"Yes, I admit that you have made a good case of it from your standpoint," she answered; "still I must say that a speculator's life would not suit me—if, for no other reason, the uncertainty of his position would be enough to deter me."

"We, of course, have to take our chances," he said, "the same as the merchant and the shipbuilder; but the risk is not nearly so great as the parent runs in launching his son on the world, or the farmer takes in sowing his crop, or "— laughing—" the chances one takes when entering into matrimony. The latter has been truly called 'the greatest lottery in life.' But as I said at the start everything is more or less of a speculation, and we are all natural-born speculators, from the youngest to the oldest, and the highest to the lowest. Your country, Lord Grandwell, contains more speculators to the square inch than any other nation, notwithstanding that the people of the United States are supposed to be more deeply immersed in that art than any other set of beings."

"Yet you are called a nation of gamblers by the world at large," the earl answered.

"Yes, I know; but that is a fallacy," Arthur replied. "To show the kind of material your people are made of I will relate a little incident Tremaine and I witnessed while in London. No doubt you are familiar with it but it will be new to the others here. A friend of mine on the London Stock Exchange, wishing to show us a little attention, gave us the choice of two amusements one evening: one was to see Irving and Terry in Faust and the other was to witness a matched race between trained spiders, which was to take place at the —— club" (naming a fashionable London club). "My friend seemed rather anxious to take in the latter; we very naturally, therefore, fell in with his wishes, although we had not the slightest idea what it was we were going to sec. When we arrived at the club we found it crowded to overflowing with gentlemen in full evening dress, who seemed to be greatly interested over the coming spider race. Bets in large amounts were being freely offered and taken on the different contestants, and the greatest possible excitement prevailed. In answer to our questions, my friend gave us an explanation of the situation which, in substance, was this. It seems the novel sport of spider racing had been introduced into the club and, on this occasion six spiders, backed by a number of well-known members, were pitted against each other in a pedestrian or crawling race—whichever you have a mind to call it. The spiders were to be placed in cages, fastened at the bottom of an upright blackboard; at a given signal, the doors to these cages were to be opened and the spider that reached the top of the board first (a distance of some six feet) would be declared the winner. Great preparations had been made for this contest, and it was confidently expected that Lord C——'s spider would carry off the prize, as it was well known that he had been training it for a long time. The odds, therefore, in some instances were two to one on his pet, which bore the name of Fleetlegs; while the others, if I remember rightly, were called Flyaway, Longlegs, Daddylonglegs, Spiderboy and Black-Jack. The spiders were already on hand, confined in glass cases, and their racing qualities were being extolled by their various trainers and owners. As I said before, Fleetlegs—a big ugly looking thing—was the prime favorite at good odds. After examining the racers I rather fancied Spiderboy—the smallest one of the lot, but a gamy looking creature—and I induced my friend to back him for first place, at odds of one to two in his favor. At nine o'clock, sharp, the race was to commence, and a few minutes before that time the spiders were placed in their respective cages. Promptly on time the starter said 'go,' and the spiders being released from confinement—amid the most intense excitement on the part of the bystanders—started to climb up the board. It seemed to be any one's race until half the course was finished, when Spiderboy, my favorite, forged ahead of the others and kept the lead to the finish. Lord C——'s Spider took second place, but there was small satisfaction in that for him, because he had backed his pet for £100,000, and was consequently a heavy loser. Some of you may think I have exaggerated this story in relating it, but Mr. Tremaine will tell you it is true, and I dare say Lord Grandwell can verify it because it was common talk at the time."

Thus appealed to the earl stated that he believed the facts were true as related, but the managers of the club had now put a stop to that kind of gambling sport. "Anyway," he said, "it does not alter the fact that America is honeycombed with big and little speculators. We may have a few of the latter, but nothing to compare with your Vanderbilts, Goulds and Rockefellers who buy and sell whole railroads merely for a pastime."

"That is because they each have the necessary wealth to do it," Arthur replied. "No one can find fault with them for pursuing that calling if they like it, and are willing to risk their money in that way. Besides you hold an erroneous opinion regarding them. They are not speculators in the true sense of the word, but rather investors, who buy railroads when they are cheap and sell them again when they are dear or unprofitable—in much the same manner that another person would buy a hundred shares of some stock for investment, and dispose of it again when he felt that he would rather have its equivalent in money. Speaking of real speculators the man most entitled to that name was George Hudson, of York, and a pioneer at the art. He beat anything we ever had in our country."

"Yes, I have heard of him," Lord Grandwell said. "He was the ruling spirit of speculation in his time and held the key to untold fortunes. He ruined scrip holders, and disturbed the great centres of industry. He possessed a colossal fortune at one time, and was really the most powerful man in England, and everybody of high and low degree ran to him for advice. He was afterward ruined, however, in the eastern railway frauds, and died practically a beggar in 1871. He would have done better to have stuck to his original calling—that of linen draper, in which he was very successful. He was three times Lord Mayor of York, and highly respected everywhere, but his thirst for increased wealth got such a strong hold on him, he finally became an unscrupulous stock-jobber, and in the end was loathed and despised by every one."

"Yes, that was after he had lost his money," Arthur cynically said, "because it's fashionable to kick a fellow when he is down; yet he did more than any man in England to overcome the powerful landed interest which delayed the adoption of railways long after their regular introduction into America."

"No doubt he did good in that respect," the earl admitted, "but his memory is entitled to small respect from mankind; his victims were too numerous to admit of that. You are right, however, in giving England the credit for producing the most daring speculator ever known. If he had been in America, perhaps he might have ended his career more successfully, and died a billionaire. Ruin, however, generally overtakes dishonest people in the end, and I am inclined to think Hudson would have met the same fate on your side."

"Very likely," Arthur replied. "The Hudson and spider reminiscences, though, should prove to you that America is not the only country to which the appellation—'nation of gamblers'—should be applied."

"You are right," the earl good-naturedly laughed. "I acknowledge that we are all natural-born speculators, and as you remarked—from the highest to the lowest, and from the youngest to the oldest; and I am sure Miss Montague will admit it."

"It would appear so from Mr. Caldwell's showing," she answered. "Anyway he has delightfully entertained us, and for that he deserves our thanks. But come, let us see what the passengers are crowding down there for"—pointing to one end of the ship where something unusual seemed to be going on, which, however, will be related in another chapter, as this one is already too long. In fact that comment might apply with equal force to the preceding chapters and, doubtless, to the ones following, as it is one thing to talk of brevity in writing, but quite another thing when you attempt to put it in practice and at the same time do the subject justice.

CHAPTER XI.

The atmospherical conditions had undergone quite a change from the morning, making it pleasant and agreeable for the passengers to remain on the open decks. The change noted, also seemed welcome to the ship's crew—a portion of whom were engaged in various games, common among sailors, to the edification of the passengers who were watching them with interest and dropping a plentiful supply of pennies, sixpences, shillings and the like by way of commendation. Doubtless in furnishing the entertainment the sailors had that object in view; anyway it acted as a stimulus, and their efforts to please, in consequence, were redoubled. The games for the most part were rough ones, and each seemed to call for the blindfolding of the participators, who belabored each other without mercy whenever they came within striking distance—their arms in the meanwhile going like windmills, in their constant search for victims. The sailors were engaged in a game of " hot-cockles " as our friends arrived on the scene—a play in which one covers his eyes and guesses who strikes him. Arthur dexterously pitched a couple of shillings in the hat placed below for that purpose, and as the others of the group imitated his example, or at least tried to—the sailors thought they were called upon to furnish increased sport—which in this case meant further and more severe punishment to the one blindfolded; that this was not to his liking was evident by his howls of pain when he received a telling blow in the face or stomach, and he presently pulled the rag from his eyes, saying with an angry curse, " You chaps be smart a hittin' a poor fellow w'ats been blinded; I've a mind to lick the hull lot of you, that's w'at I am ; " and suiting the action to the word he struck at a big red-headed fellow who was holding his sides in laughter, but fortunately before he could do any harm he was grabbed by two or three of his comrades, who held him tightly until his wrath had cooled down, which evaporated none the less quickly when his attention was called to the hat full of copper and silver pieces. Notwithstanding the harsh treatment meted out to their companion, there were plenty who unhesitatingly filled his place, and thus the entertainment —including dancing and singing—continued for an hour longer, by which time the small change of the passengers had become exhausted. This being evident to the performers, a funny little speech was delivered by one of their untutored number, who thanked the donators for their liberality, and added, " me and my pals "—with a wave of his hand—" be proud of the oppurtunitee to meet yous, and we 'opes that our doings has 'elped to pass away a tedious trip, wich would be mighty pleasant to yous, if us fellers could have our way;" and with a bow and a scrape—in which the others joined—the performers filed away to their quarters, with enough money—as Caldwell put it—to keep them " loaded " for a week, if they spent it judiciously for Saratoga water.

A few minutes later Tremaine remarked to Miss Montague—who was looking into the ocean, apparently in deep thought —

" You appear to be in a brown study. Are you trying to measure the fathomless depth ; or are your thoughts bent on something less difficult?"

Thus interrupted she looked up with a smile, saying —

" I was thinking what rough treatment those poor fellows were willing to undergo for the sake of a few shillings."

" It's the same thing all the world over," he answered ; " in every station of life you will find the same eagerness to secure the nimble dollar, let the consequences be what they may. Here they involved nothing more than a little rough usage to the sailors, which will be quickly forgotten in the division of the hat fund; but elsewhere the struggle for wealth is attended, in a great many instances, with more serious results—involving not only danger to liberty and life itself, but to conscience as well. The latter, however, with some people counts for naught nowadays; some men can detect no wrong in anything they, themselves, do, but are ready enough to condemn their neighbors under the slightest pretext—forgetting the words of Christ, ' He that is without sin among you, let him first cast a stone.'"

"Very well put, my young friend," remarked General Montague, who had come up unobserved and caught the drift of their conversation. "We are all apt to scrutinize our neighbor's actions more closely than our own; but I suppose that is due—not so much to the individual himself —as it is to the perversity of mankind; in other words it is a streak of human blindness, with which we are all more or less impregnated—some more, others less, to be sure— but nevertheless a fault common to all. I refer to the habit of condemning others, but, of course I do not mean to imply by that, that there is real wickedness hidden in the human breast of all; for some are genuinely good—barring a few faults that don't count—while some are wicked because it is born in them, and others because it serves their ends better to be so—or at least they imagine it does—which amounts to practically the same thing. I am sorry to say that the milk of human kindness, with which we all ought to be freely supplied, often runs dry at the wrong moment, leaving nothing but harsh thoughts in its place—impelling criticisms, not only unkind, but sometimes unjust. Take M. Rémiere's countryman, for instance,—I mean poor old DeLesseps. It is only a few years ago that he was the most famous man in all Europe, and his praises were sounded all over the world, while to-day his name is execrated by nearly every one. Why? Simply because— flushed with his success in joining the waters of the Mediterranean and the Red Seas, by a sea-level canal at Suez—

he overrated his engineering powers, and undertook to do something which neither he nor any other man could successfully accomplish in a lifetime."

"Are you quite sure of that, General?" M. Rémiere asked.

"You ought to know, monsieur," the General laughed. "Your people spent over $250,000,000 in making the experiment, and have nothing to show for it except worthless shares. It will always be one of the marvels of history that the French people should have undertaken such a herculean task which, in fact, had been pronounced impossible by competent English and American engineers, owing to the insurmountability of nature's obstacles."

"You must recollect, General," M. Rémiere replied, "that DeLesseps had just completed the Suez Canal—thereby cutting the Eastern Hemisphere in two, severing Africa from Europe—which was considered one of the greatest engineering feats of the world. This naturally brought him great fame as an engineer, and success as a promoter, and when he declared that the Panama Canal could be begun, finished and maintained easier than the Suez Canal, it was not a difficult matter to induce the tradespeople and peasants to contribute the sum called for. To show the faith they had in him, when he opened his books calling for popular subscriptions to the issue of 600,000 shares—102,000 persons responded and over 1,200,000 shares were subscribed for. The people had faith in DeLesseps, and he had faith in himself, although results show that he was misguided, and went into the thing without appreciating the difficulties he would have to contend with. I am charitable enough to put that construction on it, although the poor people who lost their money in the scheme are not disposed to view the matter so tolerently."

"And they can hardly be blamed for it," Tremaine said. "DeLesseps had no right to take the people's money without first having ascertained whether the project was a feasible one. At the time he took subscriptions no *complete* surveys, plans or estimates had ever been made, and even after he had gone into the matter more thoroughly, he blundered without reason. The Suez Canal is a tide-water or sea-level canal, requiring no locks, and is simply an immense ditch, 100 miles long, excavated out of alluvial deposits, the building of which required no great amount of ability, and any first-class engineer could have accomplished the same result. The great trouble with DeLesseps was that he knew it all and was unwilling to listen to reason from other engineers, who really knew more about the matter than he. The impracticability of a canal at Panama was clearly shown at an ' International Scientific Congress ' held in Paris, in 1878, by a number of celebrated American engineers, who had thoroughly explored and surveyed the different Central American routes. Those engineers presented maps and plans of the Nicaragua route, showing that it offered the fewest obstacles in building ; in fact, as far back as 1872, General Grant, then President of the United States, appointed a commission of government engineers and naval officers, to examine into and report upon inter-oceanic ship canal communication ; eight routes were examined and the Nicaragua route was declared to possess —both for construction and maintenance of canal—greater natural advantages and fewer difficulties, from engineering, commercial and economic points of view, than any of the others. These features were all presented at the Congress, but they were ignored, as DeLesseps persuaded the delegates that the Panama route was the best. He gave as his reason for favoring Panama in preference to the others, that there must be a sea-level canal, without locks, the same as at Suez. This showed his ignorance and utter incapacity for the undertaking, for, before he had expended half of the money raised, he discovered that a sea-level canal was impossible, and then he changed his plans to a lock system. But even this was found impracticable, for the reason that there was no water at the summit with which to supply the locks—the level being fifty feet higher than at Nicaragua. He then proposed pumping water to the surface by means of a pumping station. You will realize, therefore, that his scheme was impracticable from every point of view, and if DeLesseps and his coadjutors had possessed sufficient engineering foresight, they never would have wasted their time in trying to accomplish what was simply impossible. Even if the Panama Canal had been built, the maintenance and preservation of it for traffic against the landslides and freshets of that isthmus, is believed by many engineers, to be impossible. Besides the climate is proverbially bad; while the work was progressing, more men were in the hospital than those engaged upon the canal."

"Is there no hope of resurrection?" Lady Constance asked.

"None, whatever, as far as my country is concerned," M. Rémiere replied. "De Lesseps tried every possible device to raise more funds, but we had already spent 1,250,000,000 francs in the experiment, consequently his efforts proved futile."

"I should think so," Lord Grandwell said. "Besides, your government afterward had the project examined by expert and disinterested engineers who declared it impracticable. Too bad it was not done before the people lost their money; it was a case of locking the stable door after the horse had been stolen. The Panama ditch is the greatest of all financial bubbles known to history: $300,000,000 debt; only ten per cent. of the work done, and thousands of human lives, uselessly sacrificed, are all that remain to tell the tale."

"Yes; and one of the worst features connected with it," General Montague said, "is the shock it has given capitalists, especially small ones, making it difficult to raise funds in any other large enterprise. Every one, with any knowledge of the facts, admits that a canal across the isthmus of Nicaragua is entirely feasible, and can be built in six years at the outside, at a cost not to exceed $100,000,000—the same sum required to build the Suez Canal. For 400 years people have been looking for a passage across the South American continent, in the interest of commerce alone, and it is the most astonishing thing in the world that the United States, a Republic so progressive in other things, should be troubled with inertia in a matter which is of so much importance to her and her citizens. As Mr. Tremaine said, of all the plans presented at the 'Scientific Congress' held in Paris, in 1878, those for the Nicaragua Canal were the most feasible. The climate, unlike that of Panama, is quite healthy—Nicaragua being the most healthful portion of Central America; to prove this it is only necessary to state that in three years not a man from the North, working on the canal, died from any disease incident to the country. The distance from Greytown to Brito, the route of the canal, is $169\frac{1}{2}$ miles, of which only twenty-six and three-fourth miles need excavating—nature having nearly completed a water route from lakes, rivers and basins—and the remaining part to be done can be accomplished without much difficulty. The American people are the richest people on the face of the earth, yet they allow an enterprise, which would benefit them so vastly, to languish for want of funds. The United States appropriates about $25,000,000, annually, to maintain the rivers and harbors of the country for the purpose of building up her commerce; she built the first great lock in the world, at Sault Ste. Marie, for the same purpose, and spent millions in helping the projectors build the Pacific railroads to develop the country; and yet when it comes to cutting the distance, by water, down 10,000 miles between New York and San Francisco, she refuses aid for the enterprise. You can readily understand the advantages that would accrue to the Pacific coast and the United States by shortening the distance, two-thirds between our principal ports on the Atlantic and Pacific oceans, and by bringing it 10,000 miles nearer to Liverpool, to say nothing of the reduction of 7,000 miles between New York and Yokohama, and the advantages the Gulf States would gain by shortening the distances to other countries. Our States produce a surplus, and we want new markets for it. If the canal were finished, new markets would necessarily be opened to us, as the lessened distance to numerous importing countries, now supplied by other nations, would give us the advantage. We should endeavor to extend our commerce to all the civilized portions of the globe, and with the canal opened we would have the advantage of 3,000 miles over Europe for the trade of the 600,000,000 people in China and Japan and the isles of the Pacific, permitting us to sell them millions in cotten, machinery and various kinds of manufactures. The North and South American countries need the products of each other; both coasts, therefore, will be benefited by an exchange. The surplus of our country should long since have made the United States a strong maritime power; our foreign trade aggregating almost $2,-000,000,000, is now nearly all carried by foreign vessels, while it should be transported in vessels sailing under the American flag. The neglect of our merchant marine has cost the United States hundreds of millions of dollars; an enterprise, therefore, that would so promote the interests of shipping ought not to be postponed. That the Nicaragua Canal will be built sometime—is absolutely certain, but whether by American or English capital is not quite so sure. I know one thing, however, that foreigners are ready to take up the enterprise and complete it whenever they can get the Nicaragua and Costa Rica concessions turned over to them. The United States ought to be foremost in building this great waterway, because it is a commercial and national necessity; to yield control of the canal to any other nation would be a disgrace, for in time of war the Pacific coast would be practically defenceless."

"There seems to be difficulty in educating the American people to its importance," M. Rémiere remarked. "Doubtless the Panama fiasco, as you just now observed, makes capital timid when invited to enlist in an undertaking, the object of which, when completed, being the same. Anyway, the enterprise is too large for individual effort, and it seems to me your government ought to, at least, lend a helping hand—either by loan, subsidy or endorsement—which could be done without risk of loss from the misuse of funds, if the ordinary safeguards used in everyday business were employed. The United States government is very liberal in some things—for instance, in the expenditure of $160,000,000 yearly for pensions—but it is not nearly so liberal as European nations in the building of public works. Germany has completed a ship canal at a cost of $60,000,000; Manchester a canal to Liverpool at a similar cost. I understand the Erie Canal in New York state cost $60,000,000 to build and $40,000,000 more is to be expended in enlarging it—making $100,000,000 in all—yet your national government hesitates to become sponsor for a like sum in an enterprise which would be of the greatest benefit in promoting her commerce and industry in every section. You seem to have studied the question very thoroughly, General; have you any idea to what extent the Nicaragua Canal would be patronized and whether it would be self-sustaining?"

"No doubt on that point," General Montague answered. "About 9,000,000 tons of shipping pass through the Sault Ste. Marie Canal each season and the Suez Canal earns $15,000,000 per annum, equal to fifteen per cent. on its original cost. The freights through the Sault Ste. Marie exceed those via the Suez; it is reasonable to infer, therefore, that the shipments through the Nicaragua Canal would also be equal, if not greater, than those of the Egyptian water-course. Say that the first year's business would amount to 6,000,000 tons—which is a very low estimate; multiply that number of tons by $2.50—the proposed toll—and you have $15,000,000 gross earnings; make an allowance of ten per cent. for expenses—which will fully cover that item—and you have a net revenue of $13,500,000; equivalent to five per cent. on a capitalization of $270,000,000."

"Not a bad investment on your showing, General," Lord Grandwell said. "I propose"—laughing—"that a syndicate of Americans build the canal, and after it has been demonstrated a success, permit my government to take it off their hands in the same manner we worked the Suez deal."

"That would be an investment without speculation, would it not, Mr. Caldwell?" Miss Montague smilingly said.

"Yes," he laughed. "But Americans don't deal in that way; with them it's 'head I win; tail you lose.' Lord Grandwell's scheme worked all right in the case of Suez, but Yankee promoters have never been accused of being lambs."

"Not by English investors, at least," the earl retorted, "who have been badly salted with the shares of some of the American railroads upon which they have paid numerous assessments."

"Oh! those stocks are all right, at least to speculate in," Arthur rejoined. "And one of these days, as the growth of our country expands, they may become good investments. Anyway we don't propose to part with our Nicaragua shares; if Eads had built his canal we might have been willing to accommodate you with a portion of his stock, but fifteen per cent. stock—such as General Montague says the Nicaragua will be—we require for home investors;" which brought forth laughter from all present.

"Speaking of Eads," M. Rémiere remarked; "what became of his project? I really thought at one time that he would carry it through. I remember the newspapers were full of it."

"Yes, he had quite a large following at one time," Tremaine answered, "owing principally to the reputation he gained as an engineer in opening the Mississippi to deep sea vessels. But since his death, no more has been heard of the scheme to transport loaded ships overland. The idea of taking heavy ships out of water and transporting them long distances, over high elevations, does not sound feasible; and although Captain Eads worked hard to carry the scheme through, he was unable to get the necessary backing."

"It was a queer idea to say the least," Lord Grandwell said; "and I don't wonder at his failure." After a pause, he continued, "I should like to know, General, what bearing your canal, in operation, would have on the railroads of your country?"

"It is a well recognized fact," General Montague replied, "that ocean transportation is the cheapest known to commerce—being something like one to four in cost, I believe, as compared with railroads. The distance by rail between New York and San Francisco is 3,275 miles, while through the Nicaragua Canal it would be 5,640 miles. It now requires forty-six days for a freight steamer to make the trip around the Horn, whereas through the canal only eighteen days would be consumed—which is nearly as quick time as now made by freight trains between the same points. One large vessel can carry as much freight as 250 to 300 cars —in other words as much as twenty railroad trains of ten cars each. With such a showing, even with toll charges added, the railroads would have much difficulty in competing; the result would probably be a reduction in rail rates, which would not be pleasure, I admit, to the railroad manager. However, that feature would soon adjust itself, as the canal would, without doubt, be the means of bringing new business to our shores ; besides our internal commerce amounts to over $33,000,000,000, so there ought to be enough business for all."

"There is one thing you have lost sight of, General," Lord Grandwell said, half seriously. "Supposing my country interposes an objection to the United States building the canal. Under the Clayton-Bulwer treaty it was stipulated that neither Great Britain nor the United States should control the Nicaragua or Panama Canals. The Monroe doctrine, which your people are always prating about, might, in this instance, be prescribed for you by England. Didn't one of your presidents withdraw the treaty with Nicaragua from Congress on the ground that it might cause international complications?"

"It is true," General Montague said, "the treaty was withdrawn; and that excuse given for not returning it; but other presidents favored the project and foresaw no trouble of the kind. Indirect government ownership, however, such as the indorsing of bonds, would avoid the complication you mention. Besides, Great Britain has raised no objection, since the plans for building have been on foot—for the reason, presumably, that she realizes the canal would be a benefit to the whole world—as much to her as any other nation. So I don't think there need be any apprehension on that score. But there! I think we have talked the subject dry. I move, gentlemen, we hold a conference in the smoking-room; sorry it is not a resort for ladies;" and with an old-time Chesterfieldian bow, to more fully emphasize his regret, he and the other gentlemen left them to cogitate over the vices and devices of men.

CHAPTER XII.

The weather on the fifth day of the voyage was so pleasant there was no excuse for the passengers to remain indoors, consequently the deck was well patronized—although of our particular friends, only General Montague, his niece and Mr. Tremaine were there, as the others had arisen somewhat later and were still at the breakfast table.

Miss Montague had allowed Lord Grandwell to monopolize the most of her attention the previous evening, feeling, perhaps, that after they landed in New York, she would have little opportunity of seeing him, as the Grandwell party's itinerary provided for a very short stay in the metropolis—in fact he had not hesitated to put it in that way to her, and as she was naturally kind-hearted, she had spent the greater part of the evening in conversation with him. Previous to this Miss Montague had seemingly been careful to treat all the gentlemen alike;—giving one as much opportunity as another to worship at her shrine—or to put it more correctly—showing partiality to none of her admirers. This manner of treating them, while it was not exactly encouraging, still made them feel they were on equal vantage-ground. They were all more or less in love with her, although the earl and Tremaine entertained a deeper sentiment than the other two, and were consequently more assiduous in their attentions—due perhaps to the fact that they both possessed more determinativeness in their characters than most people, and when their thoughts once centred on anything they wanted, they wanted it so badly, they used all their energies to carry out their designs. Under ordinary circumstances the chances are that more than one of the gentlemen would have been smitten with

Lady Constance, as she was decidedly prepossessing in every particular, but Miss Montague's charms were of a so much higher order and her personality was so much stronger, it was difficult to think of any one or anything not connected with her, when she was near. This was so apparent to Miss Montague herself, she was always, by some device or artifice, doing something to attract attention to her less fortunate sisters, and succeeded so cleverly they were not aware that she, in reality, was the priceless jewel for which the men were all striving. It was this kindness of heart which made her such a favorite with the members of her own sex, whereas the petty jealousies in life, if she had shown less consideration, would inevitably have made her existence an unhappy one.

Although Mr. Tremaine felt somewhat aggrieved at what looked like preference for Lord Grandwell, he was not ready yet to step in the background and leave a clear field for his rival—for thus he now called the earl in his thoughts—and his appearance by her side this morning was evidence that he intended to keep to the front as long as possible.

They were talking about the concert in aid of the "Sailors' Fund" to be held that evening—an event of importance on shipboard—and General Montague was saying—

"I am afraid, Helen, I shall have to decline the honor of being chairman; this boat danced such a highland fling yesterday it will take me several days to recover from the effects of it. Lord Grandwell will be a proper substitute and I intend asking him to act in my stead;" and being one of those men who liked to settle details without unnecessary delay, he started off to find the earl.

"Too bad your uncle cannot serve," Tremaine said; and without waiting for a reply, continued, "I observe you still carry 'Ben Hur' around with you," taking it out of her lap. "You are evidently bent on reading it, but I am afraid we monopolize your society to such an extent you find little time for doing so;" and again without pausing for a reply, he read from the cover "Helen Beatrice Montague"—which had been scribbled thereon by Miss Montague, to insure recovery in case she left it lying around. "What a pretty combination of names. I am sure you must have had a hand in selecting them."

"No," she laughed, "my father chose them and I have been told he had one or two others to go with them, but fortunately my mother objected on the ground that two Christian names were enough for anybody, and any additions would be burdensome to the owner; so papa, per force, had to be contented with the selection of those two. He chose Helen, he said, because it meant 'light,' and as my complexion was then quite light, he thought it appropriate. Beatrice means 'happy' or 'making happy,' which he bestowed on me, he said, because he hoped I would be happy and make others happy."

"A wise selection," Tremaine said. "Beatrice—pronouncing it slowly—seems especially appropriate. I like it better and when we get to be old friends—I mean real old—I would like to call you by it. May I?" and with his heart beating a gentle tat, tat, he waited eagerly for her reply.

"When we get to be *real old friends*, there can be no objection," she smilingly answered.

But now that he had gained so much he was loath to stop there and seized the opportunity to say—

"I hope your idea of what is fitting will agree with my views and that the period of probation will not be unnecessarily long; that you will predicate your consent on the meaning of *real friends* and omit the word *old* altogether from our agreement, which implies long standing friendship and is, therefore, rather indefinite. Before I consent to any terms tell me what *you* mean by *real old friends*."

"Why, friends of long duration," she exclaimed.

"And what is meant by 'long duration'?" he asked.

"It might mean one year, two years or three years, depending, of course, on how often and under what circumstances they saw each other."

"Wouldn't six months or thereabouts accomplish the same thing," he interrogated further, "under the conditions you mention. For instance, if I spent two hours in a person's society twice a week for a period of—say—twenty-one weeks; would you consider that a long time?"

"Not if you were congenial," she laughingly answered; "but very long if you were not."

"Very well, then. If I can prove that I have known you for twenty-one weeks, on the basis I was figuring, will you permit me to call you by your '*happy name*'?"

She hesitated for a moment or two—evidently trying to catch his meaning; and then, not succeeding, answered—

"If you can prove it to my satisfaction."

"I am going to try hard," he said; and then pausing to make a calculation in his head, continued, "I have had the pleasure of being with you about fourteen hours a day since we left Liverpool; by the time we reach New York six days will have elapsed, which means that I shall have been constantly in your society for eighty-four hours. Now then let us figure the probation period, I think you put it at twenty-one weeks, divided into two evenings a week and two hours each evening—hypothetically speaking, of course;—that is four hours a week or eighty-four hours in all—just exactly the period we shall have known each other to-morrow—that is to say—twenty-one weeks. Are you convinced?"

"I am convinced you are a dialectician," she answered, much amused at his manner of reasoning. "If the trip lasted much longer you would make me believe—or try to—that the earth and this ship are congenious, simply because they both possess locomotive power. Mr. Caldwell has tried to convince me that there is no such thing as speculation, or rather that everything *is* speculation; and now you want to make me believe that there is no difference between one and twenty-one;" and she laughed merrily, thinking how cleverly she had evaded answering his question. Feeling sure, however, that he would return to the subject if she neglected to do something to divert his attention, she rose from her chair and said —

"Exercise of the body and limbs, we are told, promote strength and grace, and as ambulation is the only thing we can do at present to foster these qualities, I feel like taking a morning stroll. Will you join me?"

Mr. Tremaine accepted the bait thus thrown out with alacrity, especially as he observed Lord Grandwell's tall form looming up in the distance, evidently intent on joining them. With a desire to counterpoise, he directed Miss Montague's footsteps to the other side of the promenade deck, and the earl, having witnessed the manœuvre, decided to leave him unmolested for a little while, feeling confident—owing partly to Miss Montague's graciousness the previous evening—that the Earl of Grandwell stood a better show to win.

Thus left to themselves, Miss Montague and Tremaine continued their walk and conversation uninterrupted. He tried to bring the latter back to her given names again, but she adroitly introduced another subject; and, noticing this, he had too much good sense to go counter to her wishes by pursuing the topic further, although he would have given much to have gained his point. In their march up and down, their attention was attracted to a room on the deck which was evidently used as a quartermaster's supply and working room. Stopping before the open doorway on one of their trips, they peeped curiously in, and, as was to be expected, discovered nothing that interested them. An old salt on the inside, however, who appeared to be sewing a sail, gave them an invitation to enter, and not being acquainted with the tricks of sailors, and governed by idle curiosity, they accepted his invitation. Now, it is an old established custom among sailors to chalk a ring on

the floor around passengers who enter their sanctum, which
means—when successfully accomplished—that the visitors
are caught and must pay tribute to the chalker. This
dodge, after they had been in the room a few minutes, was
worked on them, but Miss Montague evidently did not understand it, and probably recalling some of childhood's
early games, the idea occurred to her that the sailor took
them for more than ordinary friends owing, perhaps, to
their being seen so often together, and this thought
gaining supremacy over others, turned the color of her face
to an erubescent hue. Tremaine couldn't help laughing at
her confusion, and guessing the reason, came to her rescue
by tipping the old tar, who grinned all over as they took
their departure. Miss Montague also laughed when the
real nature of the trick was explained; but it left an impression and an association, nevertheless, which clung to
both of them for some time afterward.

CHAPTER XIII.

As related in the last chapter, General Montague started off to find Lord Grandwell, but did not succeed in locating him for some little time. He ran across him, however, later, and broached the subject of the concert, saying —

"Grandwell, I have been asked to act as chairman of the concert to-night, and not being an amphibious creature like the rest of you I feel unequal to the occasion, and have offered your name as a substitute. You will serve, won't you, and help me out of the predicament?"

Under ordinary circumstances Lord Grandwell would have consented without hesitation, but his fertile brain immediately hatched a plan which would suit his purpose better; he therefore excused himself to the General, saying —

"I am sorry I cannot act for you, General, but as the proceeds of to-night's concert are, I understand, to go to the New York fund, it is essential that an American should preside. If we were making an east-bound trip the case of course would be reversed, as the money would then go to the Liverpool fund. As you are incapacitated, I don't know of any one who would make a better presiding officer than our erudite friend, Mr. Tremaine. He will fill the bill exactly."

The earl said this with such an air of off-handedness, no one, not conversant with his thoughts, would have suspected that he took a keen interest in the matter and that he suggested Tremaine as chairman, because with that gentleman out of the way he would have a clearer field to talk with Miss Montague.

As was intended, General Montague took the bait offered by the earl; and after informing one of the self-appointed committeemen having charge of the affair, of the proposed change and the reasons therefor, he hunted up Tremaine and made him acquainted with the honor in store for him. Fred had often presided at different kinds of meetings, and as he was a fluent speaker he did not feel at all diffident about serving; the same idea, however, that occurred to Lord Grandwell, presented itself to him and he tried to excuse himself on the ground that there were a number of older men on the ship who were more entitled to the honor, etc. General Montague, however, would not listen to his excuses, and finally gained his consent, but not until Miss Montague had also consented to take part in the performance as a singer, which she did reluctantly, and only after much persuasion from her uncle and Tremaine who convinced her that it was a case of charity. Presently they were joined by the other members of their party, which meant an animated discussion on some live topic—for the conversation usually became general when they were all together,—the ladies taking as much interest in it as the men, no matter what the nature of the subject might be, and both being clever and well informed on all the topics of the day, they were able to do their share of the talking quite intelligently. The conversation to-day hit on the coming presidential election in America, and strange to say nearly all of those present favored Mr. Cleveland—the only exception being Tremaine—on the ground, principally, that the country needed a change; and as he represented advanced ideas, keeping with the times, his election was urgently needed to ensure its welfare and future prosperity. As in the case of the electors, the majority ruled and the Cleveland contingent, being seven against one, naturally had the better of it, although Tremaine stood his ground manfully. As the writer has no wish to introduce politics in this book, nor to animadvert on the merits or demerits of the then presidential candidates, the conversation on these subjects will not be given, but before dismissing it entirely, he would like to ask, if it is a pertinent question, how many people, who voted for a change were satisfied with the results?

Leaving that question unanswered we will return to our friends on the boat, who grew so interested in the subject under discussion that they paid small heed to time, and were surprised when they found that the noon hour had come and gone—thus starting them in again on another day's run, which would also be the last, as the steamer was due in New York on the following day.

Mr. Caldwell left them to ascertain how many miles had been recorded during the last twenty-four hours, saying, as he left —

"I am only going to look at the record for form's sake, as I am quite sure that Miss Montague, who holds the highest number in the pool, has won the stakes. How will you have the money, Miss Montague?" he asked. "In large or small bills? In the sterling pound of England, or in the mighty dollar of America?" and as usual without waiting for a reply hurried away.

Miss Montague had taken little interest in the pool, as she really had been forced into it against her inclination, but now that the moment was near at hand when the winner would be declared, she betrayed more interest and was nearly as impatient as the others for Caldwell's return. After an absence of possibly ten minutes, he reappeared, but without that show of excitement which one would expect to see in the face of a winner. This, however, indicated nothing, as he was one of those inscrutable beings who rarely showed his feelings—in fact indifference on his part was generally a sign that he entertained more than a passing interest in any matter with which he had to do. Tremaine understood this perfectly, but the others jumped to the conclusion that his mission had been unsuccessful. In this, however, they were mistaken, as will be learned by Caldwell's report. He said —

"I have come to congratulate you, Miss Montague. I

found that the ship made a glorious run, exceeding your number by fully ten miles. As you hold the high number you are the winner of the pool." With this he took out a roll of Bank of England notes and some change which he tendered to her, saying, " Here is the evidence of your superiority in games of chance; the amount is a trifle over ninety pounds."

Miss Montague appeared somewhat confused, and without taking the notes said with an embarrassed laugh,

"I really don't want the money, Mr. Caldwell. I had no idea I should win." Then as a happy thought occurred to her, she continued, "I know what we will do with it. We will give it to the concert fund to-night."

The self-satisfied smile on her face indicated that she had settled the matter to her liking, and as no one interposed an objection, the money was later handed in for the benefit of the sailors' fund—a piece of magnanimity which made the captain and purser open their eyes, and called forth their praises for Miss Montague's generosity.

CHAPTER XIV.

The concert, financially, which is the main consideration of charitable affairs, was a decided success; and from an artistic point of view was also quite commendable. Mr. Tremaine primed with some statistics, furnished by the captain regarding the "Seamen's Fund," made a very good address, and was warmly applauded when he had finished. Several opera singers on their way to America gave very creditable exhibitions, and also came in for a large measure of applause. Miss Montague's singing, however, took the audience by storm, and as she finished one of Gounod's grand arias, a perfect hurricane of hand-clapping resounded in all parts of the room, and lasted until she commenced singing again. Her voice was truly a marvelous one and would have won her a fortune on any stage, had she wished to use it professionally.

Lord Grandwell had hovered by her side all the evening, and was fairly entranced by her singing, as was also the presiding officer, who kept his eyes in her direction most of the time and was impatient to have the concert end, so that he could be released from bondage.

When the affair was over Tremaine hurried to her and offered his congratulations on her brilliant success, and the profound sensation she had created (most of the people credited her with being a prima donna) and of course was congratulated in turn for the able manner in which he had filled the chair. Shortly afterward he found himself alone with Miss Montague—an unexpected piece of luck which made him think the fates were on his side. It happened in this way. The three had been talking together several minutes, when suddenly General Montague rushed up and stated that he had discovered an important officer of the

American Government on board, whom he was anxious that Lord Grandwell should meet. The earl would much rather have postponed the meeting until some other time—and his face clearly showed this—but he was too polite to put his thought in words and allowed the General to take him away—much to Tremaine's satisfaction. The latter was anxious to make his escape with Miss Montague before Lord Grandwell returned, but he curbed his impatience for several minutes after the earl's departure, rather than to betray too much eagerness or undue haste, before saying —

"I am afraid Lord Grandwell is not coming back right away. Haven't you had enough of this room for one evening? If so, I would suggest going out on deck as the air is delightfully warm to-night."

"Yes, I should like to very much," she replied, and five minutes later Lord Grandwell returned to the spot where he had left them, only to find that the bird had flown, just as he had expected. Muttering something which sounded like "confound that old General," he turned on his heel and started for the smoking-room, realizing that his rival had gotten the better of him this time.

Outside, with no thoughts to worry him such as annoyed the earl, and with the much coveted prize at his side, Tremaine felt quite contented with himself and the balance of mankind; and as for Miss Montague—well—she appeared to be enjoying herself also. Tremaine was always an agreeable and intelligent man to talk with—even when he did not exert himself to be entertaining—and most people found his society charming. With the warm feeling he entertained for Miss Montague, and the desire to win her affection, it is needless to say he used all his powers of conversation to make himself agreeable. In this he was thoroughly successful; and the thought had occurred to Miss Montague several times—after she had passed an hour or two in his company on different occasions—"how agreeably the time had been spent, and what a delightful talker he was on all topics." On this evening, therefore, they were pretty well satisfied with themselves and their surroundings. Their conversation, for the most part, was confined within narrow bounds, the subject being Miss Montague herself—whenever Tremaine could introduce anything of a personal nature—and during the evening (or what remained of it) he found a good many opportunities for doing so. As we approach them, he was again referring to her voice, saying —

"I, of course, knew you could sing *well*—as everything you do is on that order—but I hadn't the slightest conception that you possessed such an extraordinary voice—so powerful and rich, and so highly cultivated. Nature has indeed been good to you, and in more ways than one. I should like to repeat a couple of lines of poetry—somewhat personal, but very apropos—if you don't mind. Would you like to hear them?"

"I am afraid they must be very personal from the way you ask," she laughed. "If you think I can hear them, without blushing, I am willing to listen."

"The quotation is short and sweet," he said, "and I am sure Brown must have intended the lines for you, which run as follows:" repeating them slowly and impressively —

"'Nature was here so lavish of her store,
That she bestowed—until she had no more.'"

The quotation, and perhaps the look that accompanied it, did indeed bring the warm color to her cheeks; and she said, slightly embarrassed, but nevertheless laughing —

"I am inclined to think you are an encomiast, Mr. Tremaine. I had no idea you were capable of indulging in such nonsense. I shall be careful how I give my consent, hereafter, to listen to your poetical quotations. I am glad the darkness hides my blushes, otherwise I should feel compelled to go to my room to avoid being seen."

"It would be a matter of regret to me, all the rest of my

life, if I were the means of driving you away," he replied. "I am glad for my own sake, therefore, that the shades of night act as a veil over the extra coloring which nature has sent to your cheeks, and which to me is so beautiful."

"You should not blame *nature* for something she had no hand in," she answered. "*You* were the sole cause, and ought not to shift the blame to other shoulders, especially to poor nature's, who is often taxed for mishaps and misdeeds for which she is in no way responsible. Look at the moon; see how reproachfully she is gazing at you for blaming poor nature, and listen to the mournful sounds which nature herself is sending up from the sea, as a protest to your unjust accusation. Fie, Mr. Tremaine! It is your turn to blush now."

"You are mistaken, Miss Montague, in thinking the mournful sounds you hear are intended as a reproach to me. I have the sympathy of the sea because we are fellow sufferers."

"How? What secrets are there between you and the sea?" she laughingly asked.

"I will tell you of our sorrows," he answered, "if you will permit me to acquaint you with them in verse."

"Yes, if it is not personal," she replied.

"It is personal but to the sea and myself," Tremaine jokingly said; and then, after a pause, recited in extremely good form, the following sentimental poem —

"The Sea fell in love with the Moon;
    The Moon only laughed at the Sea.
And went on, turning midnight to noon,
    And silvering hilltop and lea.

"'Look down, lovely Moon,' said the Sea;
    'Behold your own beautiful face;
'Tis so pure and so charming to me
    In my heart I have given it place,'

"She looked, with a flush of disdain;
  Her glorious image was there;
And she knew—for a woman is vain—
  That the image was spotless and fair.

"And the Moon would remember and ponder
  The vision she saw in the wave,
As away round the world she would wander
  And she knew that the Sea was her slave.

"And month after month when returning
  In her full she would glory again.
Her face in the ocean still turning
  Gave the Moon a slight feeling of pain.

"Still the Sea followed sorrowing after,
  His breast swelling over with love,
His sighs waking only the laughter
  Of the Moon sailing queenly above.

"Though ages on ages have perished,
  Still Love sings the changeless old tune,
And with passion still faithfully cherished
  The Sea follows after the Moon."

After a pause, the stillness being unbroken except by the sound of the waves, Miss Montague murmured—

"Your words have a mournful tinge to them. The sea is to be pitied."

"And do you pity me also?" he asked.

"No," she laughed. "It would be wasted on you." And then realizing that they were treading on dangerous ground, she hurriedly changed the subject by saying—

"Do you realize that to-morrow we will be in New York?"

"Yes," he answered, regretfully. "I have had such a pleasant time I wish we were just starting from Liverpool. I shall always look upon this trip as the fixed time from which I really began to exist."

"Yes, it has been pleasant," she softly said, "one round

of enjoyment from the day we sailed. The time has been short and yet we have all visited so much together, it really seems as though we had known each other for a lifetime. After all your manner of reckoning must be right; twenty-one weeks on shore, with all the conventionalities to be considered, would count as nothing to six days on ship, not hampered by restrictions."

"Then you consent to my calling you Beatrice?" he eagerly asked.

"I did not get as far as that," she evasively answered; "and now I must say good-night. I think every one must have retired hours ago. We appear to be quite the last ones out;" and after a hand-shake, which occupied just a few seconds longer than absolutely necessary, she disappeared down the companion-way, with the words—"the sea fell in love with the moon"—humming in her ears.

Not quite ready for bed, Tremaine went to the smoking-room and found Caldwell, who was puffing a last cigar.

"Hello, Arthur," the former said, "why don't you go to bed?"

"The very observation I was going to make to you," Caldwell answered. "As you had the satisfaction of getting the question out first, it is no more than right that I should have the first answer."

"I can't give a reason why I have not gone to bed," Tremaine laughed, "further than to say that the time at my command would not permit of it, but if you literally mean—why don't I go to bed?—I can truthfully answer it by saying I am going to do so at once."

"Well, that is satisfactory," Caldwell yawned. "I am going to do the same thing myself, and for the last time in this cradle. Fred, do you remember the first night of the voyage, when you came in here just about the same hour as you have done to-night? I remember you had been walking with Miss Montague and I twitted you on your *penchant* for her. You disavowed being in the race then; you have just come in now, after having finished another walk—but under slightly different circumstances, as you are now better acquainted with her—may I ask, therefore, is the race still open, free for all, or has it narrowed down to one?"

"I wish I could unhesitatingly answer your question by declaring the list closed," Tremaine answered, not without some show of embarrassment, as his friend's question was rather personal to say the least—"but I have no good ground for believing that she prefers me to Lord Grandwell, M. Rémiere, or—yourself."

"But you have really entered the race to win, have you not?" Caldwell persisted.

"Yes, Arthur," the other earnestly replied, "to the end. I have gone too far to back out now."

"Well, I candidly think you are the favorite," Caldwell answered. "Anyway I wish you unqualified success. Good-night, old fellow. Remember the warning I gave you on the first night—'The early bird catches the worm'—Grandwell has been in bed over an hour, and sleep, you know, works wonders;" saying which they separated for the night.

All of which would tend to show that Mr. Caldwell did not consider himself in the race—whether from a lack of confidence in his own ability to win, or from a desire to place no obstacles in the way of his friend's success—the reader must judge for himself. One often hears of such unselfishness—in books; but it must be confessed the cases are rare in everyday life.

CHAPTER XV.

On the last day of the trip a considerable portion of the time was consumed in packing up, and in other ways getting ready to land.

The attempt to pass the remaining time calmly and in the regular routine of previous days, was tried by most of the passengers, but the feeling that they were soon to be on terra firma again, after a lapse of six days; and the general air of expectancy which pervaded everywhere, of seeing relatives and friends, after an absence in some cases, of months and even years, made the usual quiet visiting they had grown accustomed to, difficult of attainment. Now that the trip was about to end there was a vague feeling of regret that it was so, and passengers who had been counting the intervening days as so many months, were half inclined to wish that the time for disembarking were not so near at hand. This wish was certainly shared in by the passengers whom the writer, at various times, has designated "our friends," with the possible exception of General Montague, who felt more comfortable on shore. It is not overstating it to say that probably no party ever crossed the ocean, where each of the members comprising it were banded together so closely in good fellowship, and where each was so congenial to the other. It is true, there was a smothered sort of feeling of rivalship among the gentlemen for Miss Montague's favor—more particularly between the earl and Tremaine—but none of them permitted this feeling to rise above the surface, consequently they all appeared to be the best of friends, and I am inclined to think that there was really little or no deception practised. In the various discussions each took a prominent part, and the intelligent manner in which they expressed themselves would seem to entitle each to the same amount of space in order to give them equal prominence. To have done this would have required the lengthening of previous chapters to twice their present size, or the insertion of new ones, which would hardly be warrantable in view of the fact that the chapters are already too long, and the time it has taken to make the trip—as measured by the time required to read the foregoing pages—has seemed almost interminable, especially in these days of swift passages. The friends of Lady Constance—and M. Rémiere also—may entertain notions that those two people have been slighted, inasmuch as more space has been given to Miss Montague and some of the other characters; if so they must put it down to the reason given above and not to any desire on the writer's part to belittle either of them because his relations with both (under different names) have always been and are still of the most cordial nature, as I trust they will continue for all time to come.

In a work of fiction, where the characters exist only in name—really dummies—an explanation, or apology, such as the above would not be necessary; but in writing a true story where the characters are necessarily real (under fictitious names, of course) it is a difficult matter to avoid skating on thin ice at times;—by which is meant the danger of making them say or do something which, for obvious reasons, they would prefer not to have published. I have endeavored to avoid this, and sincerely hope I have succeeded, as it is clearly my desire not to put anything in which could, in the least manner, prove objectionable to any of them.

With this further explanation out of the way, the reader is again invited to board the ship—but for a short time only—as the voyage is practically ended, and the balance of the story to be told covers what took place subsequently in New York.

The intervening time on shipboard passed pleasantly enough for our friends, but hardly in as enjoyable manner as on previous days, owing to the fact (as before stated) that their thoughts were divided—partly on what was transpiring on the vessel, and partly on what would take place when they reached their homes—which made it difficult to carry on a protracted conversation on a given subject, such as they had all grown accustomed to. The change of dress from ship clothes to others more in keeping with the style worn on shore, also caused a slight feeling of constraint, as it changed something in the appearance they had each grown accustomed to. It is strange what a difference even the substitution of a hat for a cap will do in this respect. After seeing a person wear a yachting cap constantly during the voyage and then have him appear in a derby or silk hat causes one to almost imagine that you met him for the first time.

Miss Montague said something of this sort to Tremaine, who, like some of the others, had been in a hurry to change his toggery. He laughingly protested against being put down as a newcomer, saying —

"If you are going to view it in that light and make me work up again from the foot of the acquaintance class, I shall be forced to unpack my box so as to reappear in my old habiliments."

Miss Montague, however, assured him that she had no intention of assuming that attitude toward him, adding, in a laughing tone —

"You know, Mr. Tremaine, you have promised to make me familiar with the subject of finance when we get home; it is to my interest, therefore, to remain on good terms with one who promises to be of so much assistance to me; consequently I have no desire to retrograde."

"Rather a selfish reason, Miss Montague," he smilingly observed. "However, it won't do to haggle over terms. I must be content to act as instructor of finance, in the hope that you will permit me, occasionally, to introduce more enlivening topics of conversation. ' All work and no play,' you know, 'makes Jack a dull boy.' Substitute Fred for Jack and the maxim applies to me."

"I don't intend dictating terms to my instructor," she rejoined. "I hope to have the pleasure of chatting with you on a great many themes. I want some information, even now, on an entirely different matter close at hand. We will soon be at quarantine, and I am told that the custom-house authorities board the steamer there, for the purpose of taking our declarations regarding what we have in our trunks that is subject to duty. I have brought over quite a lot of things (mostly wearing apparel) some of which, I presume, come under the category of dutiable. I have been told that it is customary to swear off the duties on all articles of dress, as the government really does not intend, or wish to, tax one's personal belongings. I wish you would enlighten me on this subject, as I would rather pay on everything I possess than do anything which could be construed as cheating or taking a false oath."

"The passengers will be furnished with a list of what is dutiable when we reach quarantine," he answered. "All wearing apparel newly purchased in a foreign country which has not actually been in use, is considered dutiable, although travellers usually evade paying the tax by trying on or wearing the articles once before sailing home."

"But that seems to me a mere subterfuge," she answered. "Do you mean to say that people who often go to Europe for the express purpose of buying clothes, take them in free of duty on such flimsy grounds as you have named? It seems to me our morals must be getting pretty lax when we resort to such methods."

"You are quite right," he answered; "but you know it is not considered exactly wicked to beat the government especially through the customhouse. Every one does it, and what every one does cannot be wrong because there are none to object. If the same thing occurred in a common everyday business transaction, it might be called cheating, with a species of perjury added thereto, but nine out of ten people on this very vessel have articles which, properly speaking, are subject to duty; some of them having gone abroad for the express purpose of replenishing their wardrobes, and yet they will unhesitatingly swear that their trunks contain nothing which Uncle Sam has a right to be interested in. However, Miss Montague, your wearing apparel is not dutiable, because you have been residing in a foreign country for several years, and are therefore exempt, as you had to purchase your clothes there."

A few hours later the steamer arrived at quarantine, and with few exceptions—as Tremaine had said would be the case—the passengers took an oath that they had brought over nothing dutiable. It would seem that a tariff law which has such a pernicious influence in making people do wrong, and which is really non-operative as far as it applies to the personal outfit of a person, should either be abolished or amended in such a form that the object for which it was enacted might properly be accomplished. Wearing apparel brought over by a person for his (or her) own use ought to be on the free list, but as there seems to be an objection to that, the provisions of the law ought to be carried out and the methods now in vogue to evade them made less easy to accomplish. This, in a measure, could be done by having articles of dress tagged with the maker's name bearing the date of delivery; those having an American mark being admitted, of course, free of duty, while those with a foreign tag attached, bearing a recent date, would be subjected to the regular tax called for under the tariff existing. No doubt a great many obstacles would be met in the carrying out of such a plan, and cheating in some form would still be attempted—as the world is full of people who live by their wits—but nine out of ten persons, who now indulge in the practice, would be deterred from so doing and their consciences benefited to that extent.

CHAPTER XVI.

Rough weather, during part of the voyage, retarded the vessel to such an extent it was found impossible to get over the bar before sundown. The passengers, therefore, had to make up their minds to another night on board, much to their annoyance, and the captain's also. With the exception of General Montague, who was fuming and fretting at the delay, our friends had accepted the situation gracefully, and were settling themselves down for a comfortable evening when presently they heard some one shout, "Is General Montague on board?" An answering shout in the affirmative, with an inquiry as to what was wanted brought back the intelligence that General Montague's private yacht was alongside ready to take them ashore. The General had some difficulty in getting permission from the health officer, who was still on board, to land his party that night, owing to the fact that several steamers, recently arrived, had brought over some cases of Asiatic cholera. General Montague's high standing in the business world, however, together with a statement from the ship's surgeon that there was no sickness of any kind on board, gained from the officer a reluctant consent which was no sooner gained than the general joyfully bundled his party (including Fred and Arthur) on to his yacht, and shortly afterward they were landed on the dock at the foot of 23d street.

A carriage was quickly procured for the four persons in Lord Grandwell's party, which took them to the hotel they had decided upon; and another one accommodated the Montagues, Caldwell and Tremaine—the General insisting upon the latter two getting into his carriage, telling them he would put them down at their homes. The Montagues occupied one of the palaces on Fifth avenue, for which that

street is noted. During the latter part of the lifetime of
Miss Montague's father, her uncle had made his home with
them, as had also a widowed sister of the general's (Mrs.
von Spraker) who moved in and took charge of the Montague establishment shortly after the death of Helen's
mother, a matter of ten years before this story opens. At
Miss Montague's earnest solicitation her uncle and aunt
had continued to occupy her house during her absence
abroad, and the arrangement then entered into was still to
continue in force. Mrs. von Spraker was quite well off—
having inherited a large sum of money from her husband—
but as she had no children of her own, she preferred residing
with her niece rather than set up an establishment of her
own. Besides it was necessary for Miss Montague to have
some one to matronize her, and to introduce her into fashionable society, and in this particular it would have been
difficult to find a person so well adapted. Mrs. von Spraker had spent the greater part of her lifetime in New York,
Newport and other fashionable resorts, and she occupied as
high a position in the social world as the firm of Montague
Bros. & Co. did in the world of finance. Miss Montague,
therefore, under her aunt's guidance, was bound to see
society in all its glory, and from the descriptions heretofore
given of her, the reader can imagine the kind of reception
she was likely to receive from the fashionable set—of which
her aunt was one of the leaders. Miss Montague and her
uncle had given the Grandwell party the most cordial kind
of invitation to domicile with them during their stay in
New York, but the earl declined their hospitality from a
sense of delicacy, feeling that a visit from four people at
this time might be inopportune, as the Montagues themselves
had only arrived home after a long absence, and might wish
to be left to themselves for a few days. He and the others
promised, however, to make them a visit when they returned
to New York on their way home. The earl had arranged
their itinerary before leaving England, which provided for

a very short stay in Gotham, as he desired to fully explore other scenes first.

Having landed our friends on shore and escorted the earl and his party to their hotel, the General and his niece to their residence where Mrs. von Spraker joyfully received them, and Messrs. Tremaine and Caldwell to the former's home where a hearty welcome awaited, we will say goodnight to them and give them a chance to get rid of their sea-legs before making them do duty on shore.

END OF PART I.

PART II.

CHAPTER I.

The separating of the persons we have been wont to call our friends, as related in the preceding chapter—after treating of them collectively for such a long time, owing to their being altogether—makes it more difficult to follow them now they are on shore. As the members of Lord Grandwell's party are guests of the nation—so to speak—it is fitting that our first call should be upon them. Having followed out that idea, we find ourselves around eleven o'clock at their hotel, and after sending up our cards we are ushered into Lady Constance's private parlor, where she and the others of the party are entertaining Miss Montague, Mrs. von Spraker and General Montague, who have just called.

Messrs. Caldwell and Tremaine had felt it incumbent upon themselves to go down to Wall street to ascertain what the "bulls" and "bears" had been doing during their absence, intending to call on the Grandwells in the afternoon. On Lady Constance's table stood two baskets of flowers with their cards attached thereto, which they had thoughtfully sent to her. As we enter her parlor we hear Lady Constance saying nice things of them in appreciation of their kindness, and Mrs. von Spraker adds a good word for Arthur, whom she characterizes as "a splendid young man and a great favorite in society." As she said this she scrutinized her niece closely through a lorgnette—which she constantly used, not on account of dim sight, but from force of habit—and as her niece seemed to take no especial interest in the feeler which she had purposely put out, (in fact the lorgnette ought to have been directed at Lady Constance, whose face betokened a much keener interest) she said, "By the way, Helen, who is this Mr. Tremaine, who came over with you? I don't think I know him." This time the lorgnette gave somewhat better service, and the practiced eye of Mrs. von Spraker behind it saw unmistakable signs that her niece was more interested, which was not pleasing intelligence to her, as she had quite made up her mind that the Earl of Grandwell was a most desirable *parti*. If the poor lady had only known that her niece had actually refused the opportunity of becoming a real princess the chances are that a cataleptic fit would have deprived her of her senses, as she had a great liking for anything that smacked of royalty or nobility.

Her question concerning Tremaine did not really have the effect of causing Miss Montague to betray any sign that could be construed as a puissant symptom of love; but her aunt had heard, through the General, that Mr. Tremaine had been rather attentive coming over, and was half inclined to think that her niece liked him better than Lord Grandwell.

All unconscious of the thoughts which were troubling her aunt's brain, Miss Montague said —

"No, I don't think you know him, Aunt Charlotte. He is a very intimate friend of Mr. Caldwell's; but is not, I believe, what you would term a society man. He is down on Wall street somewhere—a member of the Stock Exchange. You will soon meet him, however, as you know he and Mr. Caldwell dine with us this evening. It will almost seem like being on the ship again, won't it?" addressing Lady Constance, "to have our party reunited." This was in reference to an arrangement made by Miss Montague to have her late associates on the ship dine at her house.

"Yes, indeed," Lady Constance replied, "and so nice of you to bring it about. Mr. Tremaine is a very intelligent and agreeable man, Mrs. von Spraker, and you are sure to like him."

Mrs. von Spraker, however, had already made up her

mind that her society list was large enough without his name, but she was careful not to give voice to that thought, and merely observed aloud that no doubt he was all that was desirable, but she always liked to meet a person before forming an opinion regarding him as she found very often that her ideas and other people's did not coincide. Presently, as if wishing to change the subject, she said —

"It is considered the proper thing, I believe, Lord Grandwell, to ask a newly arrived person to our shores what he thinks of our country. First impressions, you know, very often do more to bias one's mind in favor of or against a thing than almost anything else. You, of course, have had little opportunity, as yet, to form an opinion; but has the first glance been one of approval?"

"As you remarked, Mrs. von Spraker," the earl answered, "my stay has been too inconsequential to form much of an opinion; anything of that nature, therefore, expressed by me now would have little weight in my own or anybody else's estimation. M. Rémiere and I spent a couple of hours after breakfast hurriedly inspecting the residences on Fifth avenue, and in getting our bumps of localities in working order, so that we can go about without fear of walking into the rivers in the evening. Manhattan Island, as it is called, seems to be specially designed by nature for a large city, and the little we have seen of it has impressed both M. Rémiere and myself favorably. The architectural style of your dwelling houses, for a large city, is very good indeed, and taken altogether they present a fine appearance, but not handsome owing to their similarity of construction. We looked over a large map of the city last evening which an attaché of the hotel furnished, and judging from the manner in which the streets are numbered and arranged, it seems to me there is no possible chance for any one to get actually lost. A pedestrian in London or Paris, not familiar with the localities, can start out at almost any given point, and in fifteen minutes time lose himself completely, owing to the angularity of the streets and the manner in which they intersect each other. This is especially so as regards London; but in New York the streets are so laid out that the avenues and side streets, taken together, seem to form right-angles; and as they are numerally arranged, it is difficult to see how a person can go astray."

"I am glad you are so favorably impressed," General Montague said. "I hope your further investigations will tend to strengthen your first ideas."

"I feel confident of liking your country," Lord Grandwell replied. "But it seems to me the gentlemen running your newspapers ought to curb their curiosity sufficiently to admit of a foreigner being here a few hours without sending a dozen reporters to interview him the moment his name appears on the hotel register. Such thing would not occur in London."

"No, perhaps not," the General laughed; "but you must recollect that you are in a live country where the people insist upon having all the news. Your name is well known to a great many Americans who would like to hear your views on some of the important questions of the day. The journalistic writers know this, and as they are always on the lookout for good material with which to fill their papers, they called upon you for the purpose of securing an interview. I think you said a dozen reporters called; you ought to feel highly complimented then, Grandwell, because that represents nearly all the daily journals in the city, and shows that they consider you a big fish worth capturing. I hope you did not turn them away without according them an interview. Several energetic fellows learned that I arrived last evening, and before I had finished my dinner their cards were presented, accompanied with a request for a few minutes of my time, as they wished to learn something regarding my trip abroad. I complied with their request, not knowing I could furnish them with anything worth reading; but it seems the clever fellows drew a lot of information from me, which they artistically put together and published in their morning editions;" and the General picked up a paper from a large assortment lying on the table, containing the interview in question, to which he pointed with pardonable pride.

"Yes, I discovered the article," Lord Grandwell replied, "and of course found it very readable—as anything coming from you"—bowing—"could not be otherwise. Leaving your interview out of the question, however, I must confess the general make-up of your journals from what I have seen of them—does not impress me favorably as compared with the standard papers at home. The American press seems to go in for the lighter topics of the day, and judging from the samples furnished their readers in this morning's editions, I should say they were given to sensationalism, and pandered to the weak side of human nature, rather than in an effort to cultivate and enrich the mind in such things as art, science and literature."

"Why, Grandwell!" the General exclaimed, "you don't mean to say you find our daily journals less interesting than the London dailies? To be quite candid I found the tone of your papers just a trifle heavy to digest comfortably. But I suppose the difference of opinion comes from the different manner in which we live. Your countrymen believe in taking a light breakfast on cold meat, or something of the kind, and therefore require heavy reading to go with it, to supply the deficiency; now the Americans, as a rule, enjoy a hearty breakfast (those who don't are not in good health) and consequently prefer the news of the day served in such shape that they can digest both comfortably at one and the same time. The heavy literature, they get from the magazines later in the day, after partaking of a light lunch. Fancy reading a scientific monthly with one's breakfast," and the General laughed heartily at the thought, in which the others joined.

After a slight pause Lord Grandwell said —

"You have stated the case correctly, General, which, boiled down, means that the average American would rather overload his stomach than fill the cells of his brain with knowledge," and this time the earl started the laugh which followed. Continuing, he said, " I am not familiar with the manner in which your dailies are edited, but I am conversant with the workings of the London press. For instance, the *Times* employs only the highest talent in the market—every writer being distinguished in his line of work. Another feature is the manner in which they control the pens of all the noted men extant. Just as soon as a man becomes celebrated in the arts, the sciences, in politics, or in literature, the *Times* people secure him under written contract, if possible, to furnish them with such articles as they may call for, stipulating that he must not write for any of the other London papers. They, of course, pay well for such articles, and in addition agree to give the person signing twenty guineas per annum as long as the agreement remains in force, whether he is called upon to write or not. Your poet—Longfellow—was under contract, I believe; and a number of Americans now living are similarly bound. It is such things as these that make the *Times* great, and causes it to be quoted in all the civilized parts of the world."

"It is a very wonderful paper," the General admitted; "but I prefer our own papers for steady reading, and I venture to say if the London *Times* got out an edition everyday in New York—on the lines followed in England —it would have the smallest circulation of any journal published here. We all admit its greatness but it does not suit us; our minds may be perverted, but we want something that is done up in small parcels, light in weight, that every one can tackle without getting tired, rather than long-winded articles, wrapped in four thicknesses of heavy material, which only a few have the time or really care to peruse. We are busy people over here, Grandwell, which reminds me that I must go down to Wall street. You and Rémiere, with the ladies, are coming down this afternoon, I think you said; I have, therefore, ordered my coachman to be here at one o'clock, and he will get you down in time to inspect the 'bulls' and 'bears';" saying which the General took his departure.

CHAPTER II.

The few days which the Earl of Grandwell and his party spent in New York were consumed in leisurely sight-seeing—the Montagues, together with Messrs. Caldwell and Tremaine, assisting them to the fullest possible extent in that and other ways, in an endeavor to make the time pass pleasantly. Dinner and theatre parties were arranged for every evening, so that their stay went quickly enough—especially to Lord Grandwell who passed the greater part of his time in Miss Montague's company. In the daytime he had the field all to himself, as Mr. Tremaine had to attend to business; and in the evening he also managed to command the most of her attention, to the exclusion of her other admirers—Mrs. von Spraker artfully arranging everything to further this result. Tremaine made several ineffectual attempts to frustrate the earl's efforts to monopolize her society, but the forces working against him were too puissant to overcome, and without clearly understanding the reason therefor, he generally found himself in the company of Mrs. von Spraker who seemed to single him out to take her in to dinner, and to act as her escort in going to and returning from the theatres. Tremaine, of course, did not like this arrangement; but he had to make the most of it, and consoled himself with the thought that Lord Grandwell would soon be out of the way.

The earl, thus left to himself, missed no opportunity to commend himself to Miss Montague's favor, and he tried in various ways to prepare her mind and heart to receive and accept a proposal of marriage from him. On this point, however, she showed so much obtuseness—or acuteness (the earl did not know which) in changing the conversation, as if by accident, to other themes, he was forced to the conclusion that he would only be jeopardizing his ultimate chances by bringing matters to a crisis now. He also argued that if Miss Montague entertained any feeling for him beyond that of ordinary friendship, she would be apt to more fully realize it after he had taken his departure; while on the other hand, if she did not care for him sufficiently to become his wife, it would only be a mortification to him, and a waste of his time to make her an offer. This sensible way of reasoning the matter carried the day, and saved Miss Montague the trouble (a happier word might perhaps be used) of deciding whether she wished to lose her maiden identity and become the Countess of Grandwell.

The earl would have liked to prolong his stay in New York a few days more, but as their plans were all arranged, and M. Rémiere was anxious to start, he could offer no satisfactory excuse for delay; consequently at the end of ten days he and the other members of his group terminated their extremely short visit and started for new scenes—much to the regret of Mrs. von Spraker, it must be said, who would have liked to postpone their departure in the hope that her niece and Lord Grandwell might shortly arrive at some definite understanding. She consoled herself with the thought, however, that the earl would be back in a few months; and in the meantime she would do all she could to further his suit, by showing her niece the advantages to be gained by such an alliance. She had to confess to herself that Mr. Tremaine was fully the earl's equal in everything except position; and in her self-imposed task of entertaining him—in order that the earl might have a clearer field to strengthen and entrench his position—she had found him a clever and agreeable person to talk with. The question of social standing, however, outweighed every other consideration, and she determined to keep Mr. Caldwell's friend as much in the background as possible. It will be seen, therefore, that Tremaine's sailing course was not likely to be as free from obstruction as he had anticipated it would be when the earl took his departure.

CHAPTER III.

THOROUGHLY unconscious of Mrs von Spraker's plans concerning himself and the designs contemplated for her niece's future, Tremaine attended to his daily duties in a happy frame of mind, and notwithstanding Mrs. von Spraker's obstructionary tactics to prevent his seeing too much of Miss Montague, he managed to be in her society quite often, as that young lady was more in earnest than ever to master the intricacies of finance and to make herself familiar with the duties incumbent upon the manager of a large estate. In this undertaking she needed assistance from somebody, and although her uncle was well informed on such matters, she found that he had too much on his mind regarding his own business affairs, which were very extensive, to attend to her. Besides, when she broached the subject to him, he good-naturedly pooh-poohed the idea—telling her "young ladies were not meant for business, and that they were intended as ornaments in society." Miss Montague, therefore, was forced to acquire her knowledge from other sources, and as Mr. Tremaine was not only able, but willing, to assist her, she naturally accepted his aid. "A strange notion," I think I hear the reader say, "that she should have bothered her head about business affairs when General Montague was there to look after them." This may appear so to the ordinary reader; but he must recollect that the "Fortuna" in this work—not only possessed all the faculties and genius with which the goddess of fortune, bearing that name, was endowed—but not being blind, she was able to accomplish even more than the illustrious Grecian of mythological fame; she, therefore, took upon herself responsibilities which an ordinary mortal in her position would have shirked.

As time passed on, with Tremaine's help, she little by

little became more familiar with the business problems which one meets with in everyday life, and which most women find so difficult to comprehend. Her knowledge, however, was not gained without considerable hard study. Shortly after the Grandwells' departure, she set to in earnest, and a portion of each day was spent in poring over "Poor's Manual," in reading various financial and commercial articles selected by her instructor, and in digesting the daily market reports. The General occasionally took a day off from business, and seldom if ever left the house before eleven o'clock; for his convenience, therefore, and in order to keep posted on what was transpiring on the "street," he had stock and news tickers placed in his library. This arrangement enabled Miss Montague to also keep posted, and she soon became as conversant with stock and bond values as the regular *habitué* of Wall street offices, and often surprised the General and Tremaine by her knowledge of what was going on. Her study of Poor's big railroad manual also bore good results. The capitalization, bonded and floating indebtedness, and mileage of each of the important railroad systems, was carefully looked into—as well as the results derived from their operations. As the combined mileage of the railroads in the United States figures for something like 180,000 miles, it will be seen what a formidable task she had in hand. Miss Montague, however, was not one of the kind to drop a thing after she had once taken it up, especially as her aunt and uncle poked all manner of fun at her, and prophesied that she would soon grow tired of her self-imposed task and be glad to relinquish it. She therefore persevered, day after day, and although she often had a headache as a result of hard study, she showed no signs of being vanquished. It must not be thought, however, that all of her time was spent in this way, because a good part of it was necessarily consumed in attending to her social duties. Mrs. von Spraker was too much of a believer in social pleasures not to impress upon her niece the importance of keeping up her end in the fashionable world. Miss Montague, therefore, had taken her part in the social events of the season, and it is needless to say her part was a very prominent one. Being highly connected, possessing extraordinary beauty and great intelligence of mind, and the owner of a fortune estimated at fifty millions—naturally made her an important personage whom every one delighted to honor, and attentions were showered on her from all sides. It will be seen from this that she had little spare time to herself, especially as she took a prominent part in various kinds of charitable work. Like all large cities, New York has her share of destitute persons who live by the hand of charity. Miss Montague was not long in discovering this, and as her bump of benevolence was as large, in proportion, as her fortune, she gave with an unstinted hand, and in consequence many poor creatures' lives were made less miserable. She did not stop at bestowing alms, however, but in addition devoted two days a week in visiting the poorest classes and ascertaining for herself where misery dwelled. Many persons were actually saved from atrophy by her timely appearance, and as a consequence blessed the angel who had succored them. These facts are only given to show what a busy person Miss Montague really was. She believed in the scriptural saying, "Let not thy left hand know what thy right hand doeth," and the veil of secrecy, which shrouded her benevolent acts, would not now be lifted were it not for the writer's desire to show what a busy creature she really was.

Mrs. von Spraker and General Montague both told her she was overdoing it, and jestingly added that her face would become rugose before she reached thirty if she did not desist; and even Tremaine and Caldwell told her she was doing too much; but she only laughed at their remonstrances, saying, "If I find I have undertaken too much, I can easily forego some of my social duties"; to which Mrs. von Spraker, of course, entered a vigorous protest.

Miss Montague thus kept on as before, and her uncle was soon forced to acknowledge that she had studied to good purpose. He deigned now and then to discuss this and that railroad with her; and to test her judgment would often ask her if she considered such and such a bond a desirable investment, and after receiving her answer, would call for her reasons. Miss Montague had a very retentive memory, and her mind, in consequence, was "chock full" of points on railroad securities gleaned from the railroad manual which Tremaine had thoroughly explained; she was generally able, therefore, to back her opinions with reasons which her uncle admitted were sound, and forced from him an acknowledgment that she possessed most excellent judgment.

General Montague never did anything by halves, and having admitted this much, he was quite willing to acknowledge that his niece was capable of taking a hand in the management of her own affairs. This idea no sooner occurred to him than he suggested it to her; and as Miss Montague had that object in view from the first, she readily fell in with his wishes. He explained to her that her estate was a very large one; it was quite essential, therefore, that she should have some one to assist her and he would undertake the responsibility of securing a person to act as her private secretary. As Miss Montague also accepted this suggestion the General, in due course, transferred a reliable young woman, who had been in his employ several years and was thoroughly versed in stenography and typewriting, uptown, to serve as amanuensis and assistant to his niece, who proved a desirable acquisition and helped her in many ways. The next step was to become familiar with her large estate, and this, Miss Montague found, was the most formidable task she had yet undertaken. The set of books which had been used in keeping the accounts of Edward Montague's estate were turned over to her, and with the assistance of one of General Montague's bookkeepers, she and Miss Carson (her secretary) went carefully through the accounts. The bookkeeper was instructed to report every day at Miss Montague's residence until she became thoroughly conversant with the smallest detail connected with the estate. When he got through, therefore, the heiress was pretty well informed on the subject, and the immensity of her holdings almost staggered her. She knew, of course, that she was very rich, but she had no idea that her father left her so much, and the thought occurred to her several times—"what a wonderful man he must have been." The schedule of her holdings filled a large sized book, and included bonds and stocks of all the best railroads in the country, besides a large interest in city realty. As before stated the General did nothing by halves, and as soon as his bookkeeper reported that Miss Montague was familiar with the estate (and he did it in unqualified terms) he took her down to the safe deposit vaults where her securities were kept, and had her check off the different items. Every time he would pick up a fresh block of bonds he would remark something on the following order:

"These are gilt-edged, Helen—worth 127; or this is one of the best securities on the market, and commands a large premium," and so on through the list. When they had finished and locked the vault, the General handed his niece the key, saying—

"Hereafter you can take charge of this and be careful it does not get away from you. On the last of each month you and Miss Carson can bring your lunches down here and cut coupons off," and the General and his niece both laughed heartily at the prospect.

The estate had seemed large to Miss Montague on paper, but the actual handling of the property comprising it did more to make her realize its enormity than anything else possibly could have done; and she thought to herself, going home, what a fabulous fortune her father had left her; and mentally resolved that her trusteeship would be such that her father—if he could know—would be perfectly satisfied with the manner in which she fulfilled her trust. Her ideas of what is due to charity from rich persons were liberal in the extreme. It is safe to say that the promise she made herself—to devote a considerable portion of her income to better the condition of suffering humanity—would be faithfully carried out.

CHAPTER IV.

The events related in the preceding chapter naturally consumed considerable time, and the momentous year of 1893—which was destined to be one of the most disastrous to commercial and financial interests the country had ever passed through—made its appearance clothed in the garb of great prosperity to the nation at large, which promised to outstrip its predecessors in this respect, owing to the mammoth World's Fair to be held in Chicago a few months hence. The months of January and February had expired by limitation, and the time for Mr. Cleveland's inauguration was close at hand. A few keen persons, more wise than their fellow beings, had sniffed danger in the air, and had taken a reef in their sails ready for a storm, which might or might not blow over. Anyway they proposed to be prepared for it, in case it made its appearance. Among these wise persons was General Montague, who had been through so many financial disturbances in his day, he had grown to dread them, and on the first sign of anything foreshadowing trouble, he always put his house in order and kept it so until the danger had passed. With him this meant throwing a portion of his stocks and bonds overboard, so as to have their equivalent in cash on hand, in case of emergency. Two of his famous sayings were, "Stocks at present are better than cash"; or "cash is now better than stocks"; used according to the condition of the market and depending, in a measure, on the ruling prices, whether they were up or down. At the present time the second saying fully expressed his opinion, and he lost no time in putting it into practice. The General seldom or ever disposed of any of the holdings of his brother's estate, as he looked upon them as permanent investments, and he had no intention of doing so now. This, however, did not quite agree with Miss Montague's notion of doing business, who had heard her uncle express his opinion, very forcibly, that prices would go lower. He had, besides, confided in her that he had disposed of some of his own securities (in fact he very often talked over business matters with her nowadays) and had given his reasons for so doing; she, therefore, expressed a a desire to do likewise, saying —

"I want to be in a position to buy some cheap securities when the time comes, as well as other people, and unless I have the necessary cash, how can I accomplish it? If it is a wise move for you to sell it is also for me."

The General saw it was no use arguing with her, so he let her have her own way—with the result that on the following day Frederick Tremaine & Co. appeared on the Exchange as sellers of a heavy line of investment securities; and as they kept it up for several days their selling gave rise to all manner of conjectures from their fellow members —who curiously enough traced the orders to every source but the right one—and in consequence half a dozen multi-millionaires were reported on the verge of bankruptcy.

General Montague had taken quite a liking to Fred, which meant a good deal in the way of business to the latter —as Montague Bros. & Co., had at times, some very large orders which it was their practice to give out to commission brokers, in order that the "street" might not know they were buying or selling. Through the General's instrumentality a good share of his firm's business went to Tremaine & Co., and as the latter firm now had a large clientèle besides, the senior partner was kept moving, especially as the market was more active than usual, incident to the uneasy feeling prevailing in stock circles. The gold reserves in the United States Treasury—owing to the heavy exports of the metal to Europe—were falling rapidly, and it seemed a foregone conclusion that the reserve fund of $100,000,000, which it had been the policy of previous administrations to keep intact, would soon be encroached upon unless something were done to replenish it.

During the closing days of the Harrison régime the same menace had arisen, and the secretary of the treasury then in office was considering the advisability of making a bond issue; but he was saved the necessity of so doing, owing to the banks in New York clubbing together and tendering him $12,000,000 in exchange for treasury notes. When the incoming administration took charge of our national affairs, the gold reserve in the treasury—although not in a strong condition—was somewhat above the danger line, owing as before stated, to the banks having come to the rescue; and the patriotic move on the part of the New York institutions seemed likely to find followers in other cities, if they received any sign of encouragement from the treasury department. This sign, however, was not forthcoming, and in some instances where out-of-town banks offered to exchange gold coin for treasury notes, providing the government would pay for expressage, the offers were declined. The uneasy feeling—which was beginning to manifest itself in all parts of the country but more particularly in Wall street,—grew more intense as the gold reserves once more began to dwindle, owing to a revival of shipments to Europe; but the panic, which at this time was only in its incipiency and which burst in full force later on, was held in check, owing to the wide-spread belief among financiers that the president would come to the rescue with a bond issue, and thus strengthen the gold reserve. This, however, proved a fallacy; and notwithstanding that he and his financial secretary were importuned by some of the ablest financiers in the country to announce a bond sale, none was forthcoming. Instead, however, advices came from Washington that the administration had determined to kill the Sherman silver law, which provided for the purchase of 4,500,000 ounces per month, and as the country did not fully appreciate the evil results arising therefrom, it would be necessary to give the people an "object lesson" by making times hard. Not satisfied with this, the secretary of the treasury is alleged to have issued an order to the sub-treasurers, directing that the coin notes of the United States which had hitherto been paid in gold or silver, at the option of the holder, should henceforth redeem them only in silver. In such an uncertain state of affairs—when everybody was beginning to tremble in his boots not knowing what was going to happen—the effect of such a policy can readily be imagined. The feeling, which had hitherto been one of timidness, grew into downright fright, and as is always the case under such circumstances, the poorer people began to withdraw their funds from the banks for the purpose of hoarding, and as the outlook became more threatening, those occupying a higher walk in life followed suit. There could only be one result to such a wholesale withdrawal of funds, and this quickly manifested itself in numerous bank and commercial failures, from the Atlantic to the Pacific Ocean—the like of which had rarely, if ever, been witnessed before—not even during the memorable panic of 1873, which caused such havoc throughout the land. Now that the smoke has blown away, it may be interesting —as a matter of record—to count the wrecks left behind, and to compute the damage done. The number of commercial and bank failures is placed at 17,000, or there abouts, involving a sum of nearly $546,000,000, and over 100 railroads, all told, went into the hands of receivers, representing a capital and bonded indebtedness in round numbers, of $1,250,000,000. With such a disastrous railroad showing one can hardly blame the Englishmen (although it was rather a ghastly joke) for saying they had started a training school on Throgmorton street to educate receivers for American railways, owing to the home supply having become exhausted. Opinions, of course, differ as to the real causes which led to the panic; some contending that the financial disturbances in other countries were at the bottom of it, while others ascribe our troubles to the compulsory coinage of silver under the Sherman act, and still others to the impending tariff legislation growing out of the change of political parties at Washington. Each of the above causes undoubtedly exerted some influence; but there are many people—and among them may be counted some of the ablest financiers in the country, well qualified to judge—who firmly believe that the panic might have been arrested in its incipiency, if the government had stepped into the arena with a declaration that the gold reserves would not be permitted to fall below a safe figure; and that a bond sale would promptly be negotiated before any serious danger menaced the treasury. The moral effect of this alone would have exerted a powerful influence for good, as the *scare* which followed was largely due to the prevailing uncertainty regarding the administration's policy. This, however, would perhaps have interfered with the plan the president had in view of throttling the Sherman silver law. He had already condemned it, and no matter what the consequences might be to the people in carrying out the execution, he was determined that the death penalty must be enforced. Almost any unbiased person will admit that the law was obnoxious, and that its repeal was desirable; but it is a question whether the means employed to bring about its cure were not worse than the disease itself. The millions of people who suffered from the evil effects of the panic will doubtless be inclined to think so; any way they are the ones to determine which of the reasons mentioned herein was the real cause of their misfortunes. As I said before opinions on this subject differ. Believers in occultism will always contend that the real cause is hidden from the eye and understanding, while those believing in preordination will advance the old-fashioned theory that a financial upheaval is due in every country at stated periods. For my part I am not willing to accept either of these explanations; and I am inclined to think that the deep-thinking citizens of the country will hardly be satisfied with them either.

The foregoing events covered a period of several months—in fact practically consumed the whole year. In relating them, therefore, the reader has been carried considerably beyond the point at which the chapter opens. This being so it will be necessary to retrace our steps in order to pick up the main thread of the story again.

As before stated, Tremaine's business was now developed to such an extent, he was compelled to keep on the move, during Exchange hours, pretty much all the time, in the execution of orders. As this meant increased revenues for his firm Fred naturally was not disposed to grumble, notwithstanding he felt fagged out some days when the gong sounded at three o'clock.

The excitement on 'Change—and in fact in all parts of the "street"—was intense, owing to the panicky condition of the market. Brokers and clients alike, went around with blanched faces; and a sigh of relief was heaved by all when the ticker each day sent out the final quotations, denoting that the day's business was over. Arthur Caldwell was also busy—not, however, from necessity, as in Tremaine's case, as it was optional with him whether he traded or not. The active state of the market offered too many golden opportunities to a nimble room trader like Caldwell to remain idle; he was always to be found in the thickest of the fray, therefore, and pounded prices to his heart's content. Arthur was very much of a "bear," nowadays, and generally had a large line of shorts out, aggregating 50,000 shares, as there was no support to the market, and prices toppled of their own weight. The amount of money he made in these transactions was simply enormous, and the larger his profits grew the bolder he became in trading, until his name was on everybody's lips in and around Wall street, as the most daring operator the "street" had ever known. Tremaine tried to caution him against, what he considered, his recklessness, but Arthur only laughed at his well intended advice, and continued to bang the market, right and left, every time it showed any signs of recovery. It is safe to say he made several million dollars during this memorable campaign. The exact amount, however, will never be known, as he kept the nature of his profits a secret—not even confiding in Tremaine. It may seem to an outsider that Mr. Caldwell's manner of trading was rather cold-blooded, inasmuch as he made his money, as it were, through the nation's misfortunes; and perhaps they are right, although he was a man of kindly instincts, and would rather have cut off his right hand than knowingly wrong any one. He was in the market for all it was worth, and it was immaterial to him whether he traded on the "bull" or "bear" side, believing that one was as legitimate as the other. At present he favored the "bear" side, as the conditions surrounding the market favored lower prices; but later—when the shrinkage in all kinds of values on the Stock Exchange amounted in round numbers to something like $2,500,000,000—he became a great "bull," and did everything he could to advance prices, telling every one he met that stocks were selling way below their intrinsic value, and purchases made at prevailing figures would soon show twenty points profit, all of which came true, although few had the courage to follow his example. It will be seen, therefore, that Caldwell only did what he thought was fair and above board, and should not be judged too harshly. If the matter had been left to him he would gladly have made every branch of our business industries teem with prosperity, but as that was a thing beyond his control, he swam with the tide, and in doing so pocketed all he made, which, as before stated, ran into millions. A great many people, doubtless, will still criticise his methods of money making; but I will venture to say they would have shown no hesitancy in joining hands with him if they had had an opportunity of so doing.

CHAPTER V.

The panic of 1893 would, of itself, furnish sufficient material to fill a large-sized volume, and the scant notice given to it in the preceding chapter but imperfectly relates the disastrous results arising therefrom, and the causes which led thereto. As the writer, however, had no intention at the start of introducing the subject—other than it might occur in the natural order of events, in connection with the story he is relating—ample space has already been given it. Besides, the memory of it is still fresh in most people's minds, and the present generation will need no reminder to recall the stirring events connected therewith. The panic of 1873 is still remembered by all who went through it; and it doubtless would have remained a live topic for years to come, had not the one of 1893 superseded it. It is now, however, a back number, and will henceforth only be referred to as ancient history. It is to be hoped that the evil effects of the 1893 squall to the country, will pass into oblivion more quickly.

* * * * * *

In relating Mr. Caldwell's achievements on the Stock Exchange, Miss Montague has been somewhat neglected— meaning, of course, in not keeping her before the reader's notice; for it goes without saying that she seldom had cause for complaint in being overlooked by her friends. In fact her entrance into society had been the signal for hosts of people, whom she met in her daily rounds, to call upon her; and she was already beginning to think that a little more time to herself would not be unwelcome. Messrs. Tremaine and Caldwell, of course, were on a more intimate footing than the others, and were encouraged to call often and stay long, by their young hostess, which they were not slow in doing,—especially the former, who was with Miss Montague as often as circumstances would permit—albeit that Mrs. von Spraker was not overcordial, and often, under some pretext or other, broke up his *tête-à-têtes*. He was not to be discouraged, however, by the aunt, as long as he received any sign of cheer from the niece, and as the latter always treated him with the utmost consideration, he took it for granted that his society was agreeable to her, and was, if anything, more assiduous in his attentions than ever. This state of affairs continued uninterruptedly until about the middle part of May, when an unlooked-for contingency arose which made it necessary for both Mrs. von Spraker and her niece to hurriedly depart from the city. It seems that a sister of the General and Mrs. von Spraker resided in a place called Chiriqui—about 250 miles west of Chicago —and a telegram from there had been received stating that Mrs. Palmer (the sister referred to) was dangerously ill. Mrs. von Spraker considered it her duty to answer such a summons at once by hastening to her sister's bedside, and easily persuaded her niece to accompany her. Their preparations were accordingly hastily made; and a few hours after the receipt of the telegram, they were on board the "Empire State Express," whirling through the air at the rate of sixty miles an hour. Traveling in the luxuriousness which this train affords, the journey was comfortably and speedily made—the only delay and consequent annoyance to the travelers being a three hours' wait at a station called Cahawba.

For some inexplicable reason the Chattahooche Central Railroad, although running through Chiriqui—a town of 5,000 inhabitants—had no station there, consequently passengers from the East bound for that place, were obliged to go twenty five miles beyond to Cahawba and there transfer to a little local road which brought them back again. This unseemly arrangement had naturally caused the people of Chiriqui great inconvenience for years, and they had signed petition after petition, asking the Chattahooche Central Railroad to erect a station in their town, and permitting local trains, at least, to stop there. But for some unknown cause the officials of the road paid no heed to their petitions; and this appeared all the more strange to the townspeople, because it would have been a fairly good investment for the company, and with little or no expense incurred. Mrs. von. Spraker and her niece had grown very tired of the long wait at Cahawba, and the latter had suggested the advisability of engaging a carriage and driving over. This practical idea, however, did not meet with Mrs. von Spraker's approbation, and the consequence was that when the train over the Stony Creek and Cahawba Railroad, (the road running to Chiriqui) put in an appearance, she had worked herself into a white heat—declaring that even in China, where no railroads existed, the facilities offered to travelers were much better than in America. The trip from New York to Cahawba had brought forth praises for the *par excellence* of the service, but the inconvenience suffered at the tail end of the journey made her forget her former commendatory remarks, and assert over and over that nothing would induce her to make a long trip of this kind again. Mrs. von Spraker had been used to having everything she wanted brought to her, for such a long time, she was apt to grow irritable when anything went counter to her wishes. In the present instance, however, the reader will admit that she had, at least, some slight ground for complaint, as the facilities for getting into Chiriqui were certainly very poor. This trifling incident in their journey has been given in detail for the reason that it is closely connected with some of the results which are hereafter related.

Upon stepping off the train at Chiriqui a good-looking young man (or rather boy, for he was not over nineteen years of age) who was standing on the platform evidently waiting for them, claimed their attention by raising his hat, and then introducing himself as Mrs. Palmer's son. He informed them that a carriage was in waiting back of the station which would convey them to his home about a mile distant; and then, as if divining the question his aunt was about to ask, he informed her that his mother had, during the last twenty-four hours, undergone a slight change for the better, but was still in a very precarious condition. Charmed by her nephew's pleasing looks and manner, and somewhat relieved upon hearing the news regarding her sister, Mrs. von Spraker had recovered her usual frame of mind by the time the carriage drew up in front of the Palmer residence, which was a fine large house erected in the middle of extensive and well laid out grounds. The noise of the carriage wheels brought to the door a middle-aged gentleman of prepossessing appearance, whom their escort introduced as his father, and who gave them a cordial welcome.

"It is some years since I have had the pleasure of seeing you, Charlotte," he said, addressing his sister-in-law; "and this young lady with you is, I think, entirely new to me. I presume that Ned" (meaning his son) "has told you his mother is a trifle better. Our doctor has made us feel more encouraged by his report to-day, and we are now in hopes that the crisis has passed. Mary" (referring to his wife) "has not been told of your coming, and I doubt the expediency of acquainting her with your arrival just yet as she is in too weak a state to bear excitement of any kind."

While carrying on this conversation, Mr. Palmer was conducting his guests indoors, and after seating them in what appeared to be the drawing-room, dispatched Ned in quest of his sister, and he soon reappeared with a rosy-cheeked girl apparently a year or so his senior. Miss Palmer, or Maud, as her father called her, gave her aunt and cousin a further welcome, and a few minutes afterward conducted them to their apartments, so as to enable them to remove their dust-stained garments and all other traces of their long railroad journey.

Having brought Mrs. von Spraker and her niece so far away from their home, perhaps a brief description of their western relatives and the place they resided in may not be inappropriate. For this we will take a clean sheet and break the ground for a new chapter.

CHAPTER VI.

The Palmer household consisted of four members, all of whom the reader has met, with the exception of Mrs. Palmer, who was struggling between life and death from an attack of typhoid fever, contracted while on a short visit to some friends living in a neighboring village. Mr. Palmer was a bridge contractor and mill owner of some means, and was the leading citizen of Chiriqui, having been a resident of that place all his lifetime. In fact he and the present generation of Montagues had all been born there, their parents having been the first ones to settle in that locality, and the ones who had given the place its present name (pronounced Che-re-kee). The Palmer and Montague families had both emigrated from England about the same time, and after wandering aimlessly over a portion of our broad domain, they procured land grants from the government and started in to till their soil. As the land was fairly productive they succeeded very well, and as their means accumulated they branched out in other directions—starting first a saw mill and then a flour mill—with the result that in a very few years Chiriqui had grown into a fair-sized village, and the Montagues and Palmers were the owners of almost everything in sight. In time young Palmer (who was an only child) married Mary Montague and they settled down for good in the place where they were born. As the Montague boys (Edward and Charles) approached manhood, they seemed to realize that their environments, in a business sense, were more circumscribed than they would be in a larger place, and that their chances of success would be greatly enhanced if they moved to one of the large cities. This idea became so thoroughly imbedded in their minds, Montague, senior, saw that it was useless to combat their wishes. He therefore permitted them to have their own way, and furnished them with a moderate capital to commence business for themselves. Having been in the grain business with their father, as growers, and in the milling as grinders, they conceived the idea of becoming commission merchants in cash grain, and decided that Chicago would be the best field for their operations. This idea being carried out, they were soon doing business in the "windy city" under the firm name of Montague Bros. Both young men possessed more than the ordinary amount of intelligence, but Edward, the elder, undoubtedly, had more acumen than his brother, and seemed to have the gift of being able to discount the future. Be that as it may, after two fairly successful years in Chicago he convinced his brother that New York was the most desirable field for them to permanently locate in, with the result that they pulled up stakes and planted them again in the metropolis. In starting the second time the brothers decided to add banking, on a small scale, to their regular grain business, and continued to do both for several years, until finally the new branch had developed to such an extent they decided to drop the grain business entirely. The reader is already aware how wonderfully successful their firm eventually became—Edward Montague having left, at his death, an estate valued at fifty million dollars, while kind fortune favored the General to the extent of half as much. Edward Montague made a large portion of his money in outside investments not connected with the firm, which will account for the disparity in their respective fortunes. For fear that some may not be able to reconcile General Montague's title (which denotes military service) with the fact that he was engaged in business during the civil war period, it should be stated that he earned his glory, not on the battlefield, but on a governor's staff. After locating in New York, the Montague brothers seldom visited their old home, owing to the great distance which intervened and the trouble in getting there—the Chattahooche Central not having been projected until a long time afterward. When their father died, about ten years subsequent to their leaving Chiriqui (their mother dying a year or two previous) their sister Charlotte was taken back to New York with them and a place made for her in Edward's home—the latter having been married a few years before to the daughter of one of his clients. Here she remained until her own marriage to Mr. von Spraker took place. As previously related, General Montague elected to remain a bachelor.

This disposes of the early history of the Montagues and brings us back to their birthplace, of which suffice it to say, that in time it grew from a moderate sized village to a good-sized town, and it was confidently predicted when the line of the Chattahooche Central Railroad was projected to run through Chiriqui—that it would soon become a thriving city. The refusal of that company, however, to make Chiriqui a stopping place dashed their hopes to the ground; and in consequence many invectives were hurled by the citizens at the head of the president and chief stockholder, a former resident of the town, named Albert Stockholm. The reader will learn more of this gentleman later on.

CHAPTER VII.

THE unexpected visit of Mrs. von Spraker and her niece to Chiriqui turned out more pleasantly than either had any reason to suppose would be the case. In the first place Mrs. Palmer showed such visible signs of improvement after they had been there a day or two, the doctor declared the danger mark had been passed. A verdict like this, after death had been hourly expected, brought relief and sunshine to the whole household, and even exerted a cheering influence throughout the town, as Mrs. Palmer was greatly beloved by the Chiriqui people for her many good deeds. Besides, the names of Palmer and Montague were deeply engraved in the memory of the citizens as the founders of their town, and the principal owners of all that it contained. Through their instrumentality and generosity Chiriqui had been made one of the prettiest places to be found anywhere. It abounded with fine parks and boulevards—the former plentifully sprinkled with pieces of statuary—including life-sizes of the first Palmer and of the Montague, erected by the citizens—and altogether the town presented a very attractive appearance, of which the residents were all vastly proud. It is small wonder, therefore, that the serious illness of Mrs. Palmer caused so much sorrow throughout the town, and the revulsion of feeling which obtained when the news of her being out of danger was publicly announced. It seemed as though every one in the place called to offer his or her congratulations; and in doing so, the majority of them had the pleasure of meeting Mrs. von Spraker and Miss Montague. A great many had known the former as Charlotte Montague, but the beautiful daughter of Edward Montague was entirely new to them, and they all vied with each other in paying her homage. Invitations for their entertainment poured in from all sides. The town council was called together for the express purpose of passing resolutions of welcome, and appointing a select committee of leading citizens to wait on the New York ladies and tender them the freedom of the township.

Such respectful attention could not help but be pleasing, especially to Mrs. von Spraker, who liked everything on a grand scale. She and her niece, therefore, were really sorry when their visit came to an end—just two weeks after their arrival—and they determined to repeat it at some time in the near future. Mrs. Palmer was now able to sit up, and was recovering rapidly her normal condition; consequently there was no necessity for them to remain longer on her account. Besides, Lord Grandwell's party was located at Chicago, doing the World's Fair, and arrangements had been made to spend a week there with them. Miss Montague had taken a great liking to Chiriqui—partly on account of the place itself, and partly because her father had been born there. Before leaving, therefore, she had perfected arrangements for the building of a handsome Episcopal church to take the place of the old one which was dilapidated and much too small for the congregation's needs. She also had plans drawn for a new town hall, which she proposed erecting and presenting to the people in the name of her father. In addition to this she promised to see what influence could be brought to bear upon the Chattahooche Central officials, to induce them to stop their trains at Chiriqui. She had small hope, however, of being able to accomplish much in this direction, after hearing the full story and reason of Mr. Stockholm's animosity toward the town.

It seems that he had formerly been a resident of the place, for a number of years, but finally left it, vowing vengeance, owing to fancied slight to himself by the townspeople—or as they put it because he did not occupy as large a place in their estimation as he did in his own. The story in brief, as related by Mr. Palmer and corroborated by others, is as follows:

Albert Stockholm—then a young man about twenty-one years of age, and fully thirty years before this—entered Chiriqui one day in dilapidated garments and resembled, in appearance, very much the ordinary tramp. It was only in appearance, however, for unlike the general run of tramps, he was willing to work and immediately set out in earnest to find something to do. As the mills of Montague & Palmer seemed to be the likeliest place to find what he wanted, he directed his footsteps toward them. Upon entering the office of the flour mill he enquired for the owner, and, as luck would have it, Montague, senior, happened to be there himself. The tramp visitor explained the nature of his call, stating that he had come from California and was on his way to Chicago; but his money had given out and he was unable to walk further; he had been on his feet continually for the past three days, and during that time had eaten but little. He wound up by saying—

"I know, sir, my appearance is against me; but if you will give me work I promise faithful service."

Mr. Montague was a kind-hearted man, and as there was nothing in the mill the stranger could steal, he first sent him to his own house to get a good meal, and told him when he got thoroughly rested after his long tramp, to come back and the foreman would put him to work. He then gave him some money to pay for a night's lodging—saying, as he did so, in a half-jesting tone—" If you show up to-morrow one of my men will find you a permanent lodging house, and if you don't "—here the old gentleman chuckled—" he will be saved the trouble."

There was no necessity, however, for doubt to have crossed Mr. Montague's mind, because the stranger was promptly on hand the following morning, and presenting a somewhat better appearance, as he had evidently taken some pains to remove the dirt, gathered while traveling, from his clothes. The newcomer was put to work, and as he had promised, rendered faithful service—in fact really doing two men's work—which his employers were not long in finding out. Neither was it a case of "a new broom sweeping clean," because the stranger seemed to develop more force and intelligence with every day that came into existence. He gave his name as Albert Stockholm and that was all the information he vouchsafed concerning himself; and all that was ever learned—notwithstanding he resided in Chiriqui ten years. He was a close-mouthed fellow and rarely mingled with his neighbors. This manner of living, of course, was not calculated to make him many friends, but that evidently was a feature which concerned him not at all—his only aim being to ingratiate himself in the good will of his employers by faithful and intelligent service. In this respect he succeeded even beyond his own expectations. Mr. Montague—whose sons had left him to go in business for themselves—seemed to take a liking to him from the start, and missed no opportunity to push him forward. The result was that he stepped from one position to another, until at the end of two years from the day he entered the village, he was made a sort of general superintendent of all the various interests belonging to Messrs. Montague & Palmer, and at the end of five years was given an interest in the firm. The remaining five years of Stockholm's stay in Chiriqui were passed in much the same manner as before—that is to say—in pushing himself to the front. He had previously seemed to care only for business, but after being admitted into the firm he launched out in other directions—commencing with village politics and then gradually working himself into society. No one could quite understand how he did it, but they all began to realize that he was very much on top. Stockholm had developed into a great big fellow who permitted nothing removable to stand in the way of his progress; if any one had attempted to obstruct his path, he would have picked him up bodily and pitched him over some fence. Fortunately, no person attempted this, and he was allowed to crawl up the ladder of success, picking the best of everything as he went along, until finally he reached for something and did not get it. This something was the presidency of the village which had been filled by either Montague, senior, or Palmer, senior, ever since the office existed. These gentlemen had been in harness so long they were quite willing to step down and let some one else have the glory. When this became known it seemed fitting to the citizens that Mr. Palmer's son should be given the office. Mr. Stockholm did not believe in that kind of succession, so appeared on the scene as a candidate himself. He had never been popular with the people, although it was impossible not to admire the man for the push and dash which had put him in his present position, in such a short time. The people now, however, decided that he was an ingrate to enter the lists against one of his benefactors, and they determined to make his defeat as much of a "Waterloo" as possible. To that end every person with a vote was seen before election day and pledged to support young Palmer, who was as popular with all as his opponent was the reverse. The result can easily be foreshadowed. There was only one solitary vote for the too pushing Stockholm and it was surmised that that was cast by himself. There was great rejoicing when the vote was announced, and the defeated candidate felt very bitter toward the people. This feeling, instead of dying out, seemed to increase on both sides as the days wore along, until finally Mr. Stockholm would walk through the whole place without even speaking or bowing to those whom he encountered, and his neighbors, of course, treated him likewise. Three months passed by without bringing any change in their respective relations, when the defeated candidate seemed to realize that his usefulness in Chiriqui was at an end. Anyway he suddenly informed Mr. Montague one day that he had made arrangements to leave the place for good; adding—"the people are evidently tired of me and I am quite sure I have had enough of them."

That Mr. Montague coincided with him is quite certain; for instead of trying to persuade him to stay, he made him a liberal offer to purchase his interest in the firm—which Stockholm accepted on the spot. In less than twenty-four hours he was gone—no one knew whither. Before leaving he remarked to some one that he would make the grass grow on the streets of Chiriqui some day.

The villagers laughed when they heard of Stockholm's parting shot, and at the end of six months had virtually ceased to give him a thought. About five years later the Chattahooche Central Railroad—running from Chicago to Woodside, a distance of 450 miles—was projected. The Chiriqui people were much elated at the prospect, as the line was to run through their village,—or rather town, as a new charter had been taken out a short time previous, entitling it to the more important name. Right of way through the town was, of course, obtained without difficulty, the people naturally thinking that Chiriqui would be a stopping place. Their chagrin can be imagined when they discovered their error, after the road was completed. It was then learned that the president and chief stockholder of the company was no other than their former resident— Albert Stockholm, Esq. He had been completely lost track of since his departure from Chiriqui and where he went to and how he managed to attain his present position no one in the town knew. It was surmised, however, that Stockholm started the road on cheek, pure and simple; and as fast as he completed a few miles, issued first mortgage bonds to pay for them. That the building of the road was a money making scheme there is little room for doubt. A gentleman in a position to know, and thoroughly reliable, informed Mr. Palmer that the construction of the line, including full equipment for the same, had cost about $31,000 per mile—making for the 450 miles an expenditure of, say, $14,000,000. Instead, however, of issuing only bonds and stock to cover that amount, the road was bonded for $16,000,000, and capitalized for $15,000,000 more: that is to say, out of $31,000,000 of securities issued, $17,000,000 represented nothing but water. The Chattahooche Central road after it got fairly started did a very decent business, but the chances of its earning a dividend on the stock seemed very remote indeed; in fact the company was doing quite well to pay the interest on its bonds; and it was surmised that the president (who was also chairman of the finance committee) found it necessary at times to use the concern's credit in borrowing funds with which to do it. In that respect, however, Mr. Stockholm only followed the precedent set him by some other railroad managers, and should, therefore, not be judged too harshly.

It is hardly possible that Mr. Stockholm built his road simply as a matter of revenge against Chiriqui, but it is quite certain that that feeling actuated him in not permitting trains to stop there.

The townspeople, finding that no satisfaction could be obtained from the company, laid the matter before their state Legislature, but their efforts were also fruitless there.

"A very wonderful story," Miss Montague had commented, after listening to Mr. Palmer; and she might have added—referring to Mr. Stockholm—; "a very remarkable man." He was certainly that; but so steeped in sordidness, his good qualities were completely dwarfed.

No wonder Miss Montague thought, after hearing the story, "what a waste of time it will be in trying to get a man of such calibre to do something he does not want to."

She gave her promise, however, to make the attempt and she intended keeping her word. The thought crossed her mind that perhaps her uncle, General Montague, might be able to render some assistance. She accordingly sat down and wrote him the full particulars before leaving for Chicago, so that he might have a chance to look into the matter by the time she reached home.

CHAPTER VIII.

Miss Montague and her aunt spent a very pleasant week in Chicago with the Grandwells; and, of course, were much delighted with the World's Fair—as were also the members of the earl's party. M. Rémiere admitted frankly that the great Paris Exposition was quite inferior—especially in regard to its buildings, which could not be compared with those in Chicago. Most every one in the United States visited the mammoth show at Chicago, consequently there is no necessity of going over the ground here.

At the end of a week the Grandwells and Montagues departed for New York, or rather Newport, as the latter had opened their cottage there and had invited the earl's party to be their guests.

Almost nine months had elapsed since Lord Grandwell and the balance of his party arrived in America. During that time they did the western part of the country very thoroughly—much more so than nine-tenths of our own citizens—some of whom (from the East) go abroad quite often, but previous to the World's Fair, had never been as far West as Buffalo. When M. Rémiere arrived in San Francisco he persuaded the others into taking the steamer for Honolulu, telling them that Hawaii was soon to be annexed to the United States and they had better take in the whole American show while they were about it.

They enjoyed the trip exceedingly, and after returning from Honolulu spent several months in the Pacific States, and then crossed over into Canada, working down through that country, by slow degrees, until they reached Montreal, where they remained a couple of weeks, then visiting the other important cities in the Dominion in the same manner, and finally, going back to Chicago to take in the World's

Fair. Their trip thus far had been thoroughly enjoyable and all the members of the party were unstinted in their praise of America—the greatness of which far exceeded their expectations and caused them to open their eyes. As the reader is supposed to have an intimate knowledge of his own country it is needless to add anything further to the brief description already given of their travels. Suffice it to say that they were thoroughly satisfied with their trip and, as before stated, were now on their way to Newport accompanied by Miss Montague and Mrs. von Spraker, whose guests they were to be. The party arrived in New York only an hour or two before the Newport steamer sailed; and as they had arranged to go through to their destination without stopping over night in the metropolis, they went direct to the steamer.

Upon arriving at the Fall River pier, Miss Montague sent a telephone message to General Montague, notifying him of their plans, who shortly afterward put in an appearance, accompanied by Caldwell and Tremaine. The visitors were allowed only a short time on board, as the steamer soon afterward started; but before going ashore Fred and Arthur had accepted an invitation to spend a few days in Newport, it being arranged that they should accompany the General when he went at the close of the week.

Just as General Montague was about to get off he said to his niece—

"By the way, Helen, Mr. Stockholm—the gentleman whom you wrote to me about—was in our office to-day with a view of getting our assistance in the reorganization of his road."

"Why! what is the trouble with it?" she exclaimed.

"Didn't you know," the General asked, "that the Chattahoochee Central was obliged some time ago to ask for a receiver? I thought you kept posted on railroad affairs nowadays."

"I try to," she laughed, "but so many roads are asking

for receivers this year, it is a difficult matter to remember them all."

"Yes, it taxes one's memory, I must confess," he answered; and then as "All aboard" was shouted he hurried ashore, saying as he left, "will tell you all about Stockholm when I see you in Newport."

Three days later General Montague and his two companions were on the steamer again; but this time they remained on board when the vessel sailed, as they were bound for Newport themselves. Upon landing the following morning, they found the Montague equipage waiting for them. Mr. Tremaine had never been in Newport before; the drive to the Montague cottage, therefore, which took about thirty minutes, was very interesting and pleasant to him, as the General pointed out all the places of importance they drove past. The Montague establishment, in common with all other residences in Newport was called a cottage; but mansion would be a more fitting word to describe its imposing appearance. It was one of the largest and best houses in Newport, with nearly six acres of land around it. The house of itself was quite handsome; but the perfect manner in which the grounds were laid out, containing several pieces of valuable statuary imported direct from Europe, made it look wonderfully imposing, especially to those seeing it for the first time. Edward Montague not only had the gift of making money, but he also possessed an artistic sense which told him how to spend it. He was lavish in his expenditures, liking to have the best that was going, but he never touched anything that was not in harmony with good taste or smacked in the least degree of vulgarism. His daughter was very much like him in this respect —in fact she seemed to have inherited all his good qualities.

As the carriage left the public avenue to enter the Montague grounds, Tremaine thought to himself "what a presumptuous individual I am to imagine that I stand the ghost of a show in trying to win the most beautiful and richest maiden in the whole world. On board the ocean steamer the task seemed formidable enough, but here the evidence of her enormous wealth confronts one on all sides and seems, somehow, to act as an insurmountable barrier. The odds are truly against me, especially with a scheming aunt in the background who is doing her utmost to help Grandwell's suit, which means, of course, when compared with him, that I am a nonentity or represented as such." All of which would go to show that Mr. Tremaine was a little down in the mouth, due, perhaps, from overwork; because the reader is certainly aware, by this time, that Miss Montague entertained a much higher estimate of him than he gave her credit for.

Strange to say Mr. Caldwell was also indulging in reveries similar to his friend's—with this difference, he was saying to himself, "what a lucky dog Fred is, to be sure; he succeeds in everything he attempts; with the odds fifty to one against him he comes out a winner every time. After all it's better to be born lucky than rich. Still I ought not to complain and, by jove! I don't intend to; we couldn't all marry this American Goddess of Fortune. Besides Lady Constance is "— Here his train of thought was interrupted by the carriage pulling up in front of the house. Notwithstanding that the hour of their arrival was rather early, Miss Montague was on the scene to receive them, and under her influence Tremaine's dismal thoughts not only vanished, but on the other hand, the optimistic side of his nature again asserted itself, and he was already picturing to himself future happy events in which he and Miss Montague were the principal actors.

CHAPTER IX.

Newport, as every one knows, is the scene of much gaiety when the regular season opens, and scarcely a night passes but that one, or more, entertainments are given by some of the fashionable summer residents. Mrs. von Spraker, as one of society's leaders, was, of course, in great demand at all the social functions; as was also her niece, who was made much of, not only on account of her reputed wealth, but also to the fact that she had become a genuine favorite with all who knew her.

As the best means of letting their friends know that they had guests stopping with them, Mrs. von Spraker and Miss Montague gave a reception, to which the *beau monde* was invited. After that invitations without number were received, and as a consequence pretty much all of the afternoons and evenings were consumed in attending social gatherings. The forenoons were passed in a rather lazy manner around the house, excepting when they were spent in driving; and taken altogether the days were passed quickly and pleasantly. This was particularly so as relating to Messrs. Caldwell and Tremaine who had lengthened their visit from one week, as first intended, to twice that time, at the earnest solicitation of the general and his niece, and in justice to Mrs. von Spraker it should be said that she had also urged them both to stay. The panicky feeling on Wall street, however, made it necessary for them, and the General as well, to return to the city and look after their business affairs, as everything about this time began to have the appearance of going to the " eternal bow-wows." Outside of the disquieting state of affairs in the financial world, General Montague had an important commission to fill for his niece, which involved a transaction running into the millions. This was nothing more or less than the purchase of the Chattahooche Central Railroad, which was soon to be sold under a foreclosure sale for the benefit of the first mortgage bondholders unless a plan of reorganization could be agreed upon in the meantime. In order that the reader may properly understand the situation it will be better to relate the conversation which took place between the General and his niece on this subject, Mr. Tremaine being the only other person present.

Miss Montague had thought a good deal about her trip to Chiriqui since her return home, and the queer story Mr. Palmer had related concerning Albert Stockholm had recurred to her more than once. She had lost no time, therefore, in questioning her uncle regarding the Chattahooche Central Railroad and Stockholm's connection with it.

"From what I can learn," the General had said, "this man" (meaning Stockholm) "is a queer sort of fish. He is a good deal of a mystery; but those who know him say he is a shrewd fellow and not overscrupulous in his transactions. I have known of him for several years, but was never brought into direct contact with him until he called on me a few days ago, although I understand he divides his time between New York and Chicago. He is well known on Wall street as a stock-jobbing president—principally in the stock of his own railroad—having been engaged in three or four deals with more or less success. Chattahooche stock is not worth much, in fact never had any real intrinsic value, but through his manipulations the shares have frequently sold above par. The market price now, however, is only five dollars per share, owing to the road being in the hands of receivers, and its bad financial condition. The January interest on the first mortgage bonds has been in default nearly six months, and under the terms of the mortgage the road will have to be sold under foreclosure, unless some plan of reorganization can be formulated which will be satisfactory to the bondholders. Stockholm has got a plan drawn up which provides for a scaling of the interest, funding the coupons, etc., and is anxious to have our firm undertake the work of rehabilitation. He assumes, of course, that he will succeed himself in the management of the company, and that is the feature I don't quite like, because he seems to be an undesirable person to be at the head of any corporation, and in all probability will wreck it again sometime in carrying out his stock-jobbing deals. As for building a station at Chiriqui, that, of course, can easily be arranged, as it can be made a part of any agreement we enter into. Now, my dear, what do you think of it? I am willing to do anything you say, which is paying her a great compliment. Eh! Tremaine?"

"Yes, General," laughing, "but you must recollect that she is a student no longer."

"I believe you," the General answered, casting an admiring glance at his niece. "But tell me, Helen, what is your wish in the matter? Do you want me to assist Stockholm in carrying his scheme through?"

"No, decidedly not," she answered. "It would be nothing short of a crime to assist such a man as that to remain at the head of the corporation, thereby enabling him to cheat the poor people who may be induced to invest in its stock and bonds. He is not a proper person to be in charge of any property whose securities are, in a manner, public investments. Instead of helping him I suggest that we take the road away from him entirely, if it can be done."

"I don't see how that can be done, my dear, unless we purchase the road ourselves," the General answered; "and that I take it is not your intention."

"That is exactly my intention," she replied. "I have a large amount of capital, at present lying idle which I am willing to invest in the securities of the Chattahooche on the low basis they are now selling at, and do not think there is any risk in so doing. If I could purchase the entire issues of stock and bonds at the ruling quotations, it would be equivalent to buying the property at $2,000,000 less than the original cost. I realize, of course, that it would be impossible to do that. But I want to buy all the bonds I can around 70, and by degrees take all that are offered up to 80. The stock has little intrinsic value at present, but it is worth more than five dollars per share for the purpose of control, especially as we want to turn Mr. Stockholm out. With that object in view I am willing to pay as high as ten dollars per share. Do you think my figures are liberal enough, Mr. Tremaine, to secure a majority of the stock and bonds?"

"As the matter stands to-day," he replied, "the security holders expect to see their road sold out under the hammer in the near future; consequently I do not think there will be any difficulty in accomplishing your purpose at the limits named. I am inclined to think Mr. Stockholm may be induced to part with his holdings, or a portion of them by private sale when he learns from Montague Bros. & Co. that they decline to enter into his reorganization scheme. In the present condition of finances on Wall street, he cannot hope to get any one else to undertake the job, he will naturally think, therefore, that a foreclosure sale cannot be averted."

"Oh! there will be no trouble in getting all the Chattahooche Central stock and bonds you want at your figures, Helen," the General observed. "Tremaine and I between us" (casting a knowing glance at Fred) "will shake the limbs thoroughly, and after we get through you will be able to pick up the securities on your own terms."

"I don't want you to do anything, uncle," she said, earnestly, "that will tend to frighten innocent holders into selling. I would rather drop the scheme entirely than to do such a thing. If you succeed in legitimately buying a majority interest for me in the company's securities we will issue a plan of reorganization and allow all parties interested to participate on the same terms that I do myself. At the proper time," laughing, " we will appoint Messrs Montague Bros. & Co. the promulgators of the plan, but they will have to be satisfied with whatever glory there may be attached thereto as reorganizers, as they will get no other compensation from the security holders."

"We can drive a better bargain than that with Stockholm," General Montague smilingly said. " He will give us at least $1,000,000 in new bonds of the company. However, as it will be enlisting in a good cause to aid you in carrying your plans through, we will offer our services gratis. One thing, Tremaine, she has got to pay us an eighth commission for buying the stock and bonds, as she is a non-member of the Exchange; we are fortunate in that respect at least."

Then as a new idea seemed to strike the General he burst out laughing and presently remarked in a droll way—

" My dear you will cut quite a dash in the railroad world when it is publicly announced that you have been elected president of the Chattahooche Central Railroad, or whatever new name it may be re-christened by. The press will chronicle the event in large headlines something on the following order—' Miss Helen B. Montague, the Beautiful and Talented Society Belle, Assumes the Presidency of a Railroad, etc.' For about a week you will receive innumerable congratulations from your friends and acquaintances, and then you will be besieged by them for tips on the stock."

General Montague laughed immoderately at the picture he had drawn, in which his niece and Tremaine also joined. When their merriment had subsided, Miss Montague said—

" If I cannot find a proper person to take charge of the road who will manage it for the sole benefit of the security holders, I shall not hesitate to assume the responsibility myself. Of that you may rest assured. I think, however"—letting her glance rest on Fred a few seconds—

"that I can find some one who will manage it capably and honestly, for I intend offering the presidency to Mr. Tremaine."

Fred modestly started to say something about his unfitness for the position, etc., but Miss Montague promptly shut him off by saying —

"Never mind that, Mr. Tremaine, honesty of purpose is of much more consequence than mere experience when the former requisite is lacking. Don't you agree with me, Uncle Charles?"

"Decidedly," the General answered. "And your selection of Mr. Tremaine does you infinite credit. His management of the company's finances will be in marked contrast to Stockholm's slippery methods, I should imagine."

"I am exceedingly grateful for your good opinions," Tremaine smilingly said; "but don't you think it is a case of counting your chickens before they are hatched? You must recollect that it is necessary to first secure control of the road before your plans can be put in operation."

"Don't you worry yourself on that point, Mr. President," the General replied, who was now greatly interested in his niece's scheme. "I will guarantee to have a large majority of both bonds and stock, two weeks after we reach New York if necessary. So you may consider yourself already elected, and accept our congratulations in advance."

* * * * * *

Two weeks later they were in New York, actively engaged in carrying out Miss Montague's plan, and, as predicted by General Montague, he soon had enough securities to control the situation. In bringing about such a result Mr. Stockholm was unwittingly of great service. He was greatly disappointed when Montague Bros. & Co. notified him that they declined to undertake the reorganization of his road; and after making several futile attempts to interest some other banking house in the scheme, he was forced to the conclusion that the road would have to be sold under the hammer. Believing this to be the inevitable result he made haste to leave, what appeared to be a sinking ship, and save as much out of the disaster as possible. He gave his broker an order to work off a large batch of bonds and stock, but it was of no use; the market was panicky and nobody seemed to want Chattahooche Central securities at any price. The bonds were nominally quoted at 60 bid, 70 asked; and the shares at 5 asked with no bid. The broker disposed of a few bonds around 60 and then offered them down to 50 with no takers. He began to grow alarmed, as his firm was advancing a very large sum of money to Stockholm against these bonds as collateral, and at 40 his margin was exhausted. He rushed back to his office and found Stockholm, nervously watching the quotations from the stock ticker.

"Stockholm you must put up more collateral on your account at once," he said, in a state of suppressed excitement; and as that individual showed no signs of having heard him, the broker shook him by the shoulder violently and again repeated his demand for more margin. This aroused Mr. Stockholm from his stupor and in a bitter tone of voice he exclaimed —

"You can't get blood from a stone, Goldbury. You've got everything I own, with the exception of 75,000 shares of Chattahooche stock and that, I take it, is not the kind of collateral you want."

"No, if that is the best you can do, I am afraid it is all up with me," his broker answered. "The bankers from whom I am borrowing money on your bonds will see to-day's quotation for them, and will probably ask me to take them up. As there is absolutely no market for their sale I won't be able to comply with their request. You have put me in a bad hole, Stockholm. I wish you and your account were in a warmer climate."

As his client offered no suggestion, Mr. Goldbury got angry and fairly yelled —

"Why don't you do or say something, instead of standing there like an infernal jackass?"

The words were no sooner out of his mouth than Mr. Goldbury was sprawling on his back, and as soon as he could recover his wits he realized that his client had *done something*. Regaining his feet he said in an aggrieved tone —

"Stockholm, you add insult to injury, but the situation is too serious for us to quarrel. If you cannot offer anything better, go to your safe deposit vault and get the stock you mentioned, and we will see what can be done to pull us both through."

"All right, Goldbury," Mr. Stockholm said. "Sorry I lost control of my temper, but you must confess you gave me provocation. I will be back in a few minutes;" saying which he shook hands with the broker and went to get his 75,000 shares of Chattahoochee Central stock.

Mr. Goldbury had no intention of forgiving or forgetting the blow he had received, but he realized that it was "easier to catch flies with molasses than vinegar," and he wanted that stock, worthless as it appeared to be.

Presently Mr. Stockholm returned with a big bundle which he handed to his broker, saying —

"This stock is not worth much on the market now, but it will soon become valuable when Montague Bros. & Co. reorganize the road, as they have promised to do when the financial atmosphere becomes brighter." All of which was true, although Mr. Stockholm had no idea he was stating facts, and, as we know, entertained just the opposite opinion. When the shares had been counted and deposited in his safe, Mr. Goldbury went over to the Stock Exchange to ascertain if any change had taken place since he left. Almost the first person he met on the floor was Caldwell, who said —

"Hello, Goldbury, what are you wearing such a long face for? One would think you were entering the morgue in search of a lost relative."

"You can afford to be gay, Caldwell, for you have made millions on the drop. But it is different with poor devils like myself who don't know whether they are on foot or on horseback."

Mr. Goldbury was considered a very decent fellow by his associates, and he and Caldwell were quite friendly. With a view of chasing away his gloomy thoughts Arthur clapped him on the back, saying —

"Come, come, old fellow, you must not get nervous at the tail end. I am going to turn 'bull' in a few days, and I will whoop prices up to your heart's content. What stock are you interested in? I will commence with that first."

Mr. Goldbury cast a searching glance at Arthur, and then said —

"I don't know whether you are quizzing me or not, Caldwell, but I have a mind to take you into my confidence; perhaps you can suggest something which will extricate me from the hole I am in. Will you 'listen to my tale of woe'?"

Receiving an answer in the affirmative, Mr. Goldbury soon related the plight he was in, and when he had finished, Caldwell said —

"I think I can help you. What price are you willing to sell the whole block of bonds at?"

"I can get out without loss at 40, but, of course, don't expect any one will be fool enough to pay that figure for the whole block of \$5,000,000. I am willing to sell as low as 35 if a better price cannot be obtained. That will entail a loss of \$250,000, but that is a great deal better than going under. Besides I have got 75,000 shares of Chattahooche which may be worth something one of these days."

"All right," Arthur said, "make your mind easy. I will have the whole matter fixed for you in half an hour.

In the meantime if you want to borrow a couple of hundred thousand against that Chattahoochee stock send it in to my office;" saying which he hurried away to find Tremaine. Ascertaining that Fred had just left the Exchange, he hurried over to his office and finding him in, soon put him in possession of the facts. They then went to consult with General Montague, and a few minutes afterward Arthur hurried back to the Exchange to fill his orders. As soon as he entered Mr. Goldbury rushed up to him eagerly, saying —

"Is it all right, Caldwell?"

"Why, of course it is, Goldbury. I told you it would be before I left you. I will give you 50 for your bonds, provided you will sell me the stock at $2.50 per share. Is that fair?"

"Fair," the other echoed. "Why, man alive! I offered you the bonds at 35 and would have thrown the stock in as a bonus if you had insisted upon it. Your offer is an extraordinary one, under the circumstances, and you are the most generous and fair-minded man I have ever known."

"That's all right, Goldbury; we will consider the transaction closed. You may send in the stock to-day, if you choose, and the bonds at your convenience."

A minute or so afterward the stock ticker recorded the sale of 5,000,000 Chattahoochee Central, first mortgage 5s at 50, seller 3, and 75,000 shares of the stock at 2 1-2 cash.

In paying the above price (when he might have got them for less,) it is needless to say that General Montague was actuated to a great extent by the knowledge that his niece would be dissatisfied with the transaction when she learned the full particulars—if he paid less. She had become acquainted with the methods sometimes used to shake out weak holders and was half afraid her uncle would put some of them in practice; her parting admonition to him, therefore, had been, "Don't take advantage of any one; if we cannot accomplish our object without resorting to doubtful methods, we will give it up entirely." Consequently, Mr. Stockholm was really indebted to her to the extent of $937,500; and instead of owing his broker $250,000, he had a credit balance on the latter's books amounting to $687,500.

He was not aware, however, of his good luck, and instead of being pleased with the result of Mr. Goldbury's negotiations he was inclined to grumble and accused the latter of needlessly sacrificing his client's interests. The realization that the control of the Chattahooche Central Railroad was likely to be soon wrested from him, no doubt made him more unreasonable than he otherwise would have been; anyway he was dissatisfied, not only with his broker, but with the purchaser of his securities as well, and straightway began to get even with the latter by circulating all manner of adverse reports regarding the financial condition of the Chattahooche Central, with the object of depreciating the market value of its securities still more. In doing this he also had an idea that he might injure the company's credit to such an extent that no one would care to make a bid for it when it was put up for sale, hoping before that time to be able to form a syndicate of his own, to step in and purchase the road at the last moment for a mere song.

If he had only known of the strong people now interested in the property, he would doubtless have given up without a struggle; as it was, his efforts only succeeded in shaking out the securities held by a number of frightened holders, thereby enabling the Montague brokers to pick them up on their own terms, until, eventually, they owned fully three-fourths of both bonds and capital stock. When that was accomplished, General Montague took steps to have Albert Stockholm, receiver, removed, and Frederick Tremaine substituted in his place. His large holdings in the company's securities, of course, made his task easy, and the result was that Mr. Stockholm had to step down and out. A plan of reorganization was then formulated and quickly carried through—the capital stock and bonded debt being considerably reduced—and a short time afterward the road was restored to the shareholders, with Frederick Tremaine, duly elected president, in charge.

One of the first things the new president did, upon assuming control, was to order a suitable station built at Chiriqui, and the company's time-table altered to provide for regular stoppages at that place. It is needless to say that this new order of things greatly pleased the residents of Chiriqui and did much to foster the growth of that place. If Mr. Stockholm had been more mindful of what was due to them it is extremely likely that he would have been able to retain his position as president of the Chattahoochee Central Railway, as Miss Montague would then have had no particular object in becoming interested in the road. It will be seen from this to what an extent little things sometime change the current of our lives. In carrying out his petty revenge against his former townspeople, he was really engaged in bringing about his own downfall, and proved the truth of Milton's words —

> "Revenge, at first though sweet,
> Bitter ere long, back on itself recoils."

CHAPTER X.

In describing the events connected with Mr. Stockholm's overthrow, as president of Chattahooche Central Railway, the writer had no alternative but to take the reader to New York so as to be on the scene of action. Having seen Miss Montague's scheme successfully carried out, we will again return to her Newport home before her foreign guests take their departure. The social gatherings, gotten up in a great many instances for their benefit, instead of decreasing seemed to grow more numerous as the days passed and they were feted and dined to such an extent, Lord Grandwell humorously remarked that Newport was the greatest emporium for social entertainments of any place he had ever visited. He was, of course, much gratified at the attention paid to him and the others in his party, but he would have been quite willing to have seen less of society in general and more of Miss Montague in particular, believing that such an arrangement would afford him more opportunities to make himself indispensable to her. However, he made the best of the situation, and to an ordinary outsider seemed to be with her most of the time—in fact his assiduous attention had been freely commented upon by the knowing ones of the place, and the rumor that he and the beautiful Miss Montague were betrothed found many believers, who expected every day to hear the event officially announced. As this was not forthcoming soon enough to suit the gossips, they took the matter into their own hands, and in a comparatively short time the report that Miss Montague was to become the Countess of Grandwell was given great publicity, and as an item of news was telegraphed to the press of New York where, of course, it was seen by Tremaine and Caldwell. Neither wanted to believe the report but they feared that it was true, especially the former, who felt almost inclined, in the bitterness of despair, to send Miss Montague a congratulatory message, but fortunately sounder reason prevailed and he decided to wait until the news was confirmed by General Montague, or came in a more official manner.

Those were anxious days for Fred, and it seemed to him that even a confirmation of the news would be more welcome than the existing uncertainty. There was no alternative, however, but to grin and bear it, and hope that the report might prove groundless. This he did with becoming fortitude, and even Arthur was unaware of the strain he underwent, mentally, to hide his feelings.

The truth of the matter is that the earl, at this time, had really not made a direct proposal of marriage to Miss Montague, although he had in divers ways tried to prepare her for it. She had always been exceedingly friendly toward him, but not more so than to either Caldwell or Tremaine; the earl, therefore, was not overconfident of success, but felt that such an important matter must be decided one way or the other before he sailed for home. As his visit was almost at an end, he realized that the die had soon to be cast, and he was only waiting now for a favorable opportunity before declaring himself. This presented itself one morning, when he found himself alone with her—the others having gone to the Casino to witness a game of tennis. He was too wide-awake not to grasp the chance thus offered, and without indulging in unnecessary explanations, in a few well chosen words made her understand the great happiness and honor she would be conferring upon him by consenting to become his wife. To imply that Miss Montague was not aware of the warm feeling that Lord Grandwell entertained for her would be absurd, for his attentions had been too persistent to admit of any other construction being placed upon them; she was in hopes, however, that he would perceive by her manner that a union between them, such as he evidently wished for, could not be; and thus save them both from unnecessary embarrassment.

Lord Grandwell had indeed realized more than once that Miss Montague did not seem to be in love with him, and it was due to this feeling that he had delayed until almost the last moment of his stay before putting the all-important question to her. He was, of course, aware that he was considered a very desirable *parti* by most people, and especially by Mrs. von Spraker, and hoped that would have some weight in influencing her niece, at the same time realizing that the latter was not likely to give her hand into the keeping of any person unless her heart could follow. Lord Grandwell had looked at the matter in all its bearings before proposing, and was, therefore, in a certain sense prepared for her answer which, as the reader has already surmised, was not in his favor. This feeling of uncertainty beforehand, however, in no way ameliorated the anguish and disappointment he felt when her decision was rendered —couched though it was in the kindest terms she could employ—and for a few moments he sat like one stunned, scarcely able to articulate a sound. Self-control, however, was one of Lord Grandwell's strong points, and with a great effort he recovered himself sufficiently to outwardly make the most of a bad situation, although inwardly the smart inflicted by her rejection was still keen. During the remainder of his stay at Newport he was careful not to betray by look or manner that anything out of the common had happened, and in order to keep up appearances he continued to pass a great part of his time in Miss Montague's society as formerly. A couple of days afterward his visit terminated and he was quite contented to have it so, as he realized that it would be much easier to forget his trouble if the broad ocean were between him and the being who unintentionally was the cause of it. The earl was unmistakably hard hit, but he had no intention to allow the matter to prey on his mind any more than possibly could be helped, and felt confident that he should be able in time to tone the feeling he at present entertained for Miss Montague down to one of ordinary friendship. The leave-taking on all sides was one of great cordiality. Outside of the Montagues the members of Lord Grandwell's party had made a great many friends during their stay in Newport, hence their departure was the occasion of much regret. As M. Rémiere had been quite attentive to one of Newport's prettiest belles, and the young lady in question had accepted his advances with evident pleasure, it was taken for granted that he would make another trip to the United States before a great while, and it may be added here that such was M. Rémiere's firm resolve. At New York the party remained two or three days before embarking, and Messrs. Caldwell and Tremaine both did all they could to make their stay pass pleasantly. Neither Fred nor Arthur had received any intelligence regarding Miss Montague's reported engagement to Lord Grandwell beyond the first newspaper reports which still remained uncontradicted; they were both inclined to think, therefore, that there was real foundation for the rumor. Under the circumstances, Tremaine would rather not have been brought into contact with the earl, but his relations with the whole party had been so intimate he did not see how he could avoid calling upon them without occasioning wonder on their part. As Caldwell had also taken pains to put it to him in that way he had fully made up his mind to present himself at their hotel when they arrived, even before Arthur showed him a note from Lady Constance announcing their arrival, in which she reminded him that both he and Mr. Tremaine had promised to call. Arthur was in no need of a reminder, as he had been looking forward to Lady Constance's coming with more than ordinary interest. Perhaps a word of explanation is due here before going further. As the reader is aware, he had been greatly struck with Miss Montague's beauty, and the chances are that he would have worshipped at her shrine in downright earnest if she had shown him any preference. Instead of doing this, however, she seemed to favor Fred, or at least he imagined she did, and as soon as that idea got firmly fixed in his mind, he gave himself good advice, to the effect that he had better withdraw from the race of his own accord while he had the gumption to do so. In order to carry out this plan the more effectively, he passed a good portion of his time while on shipboard in Lady Constance's company. The consequence was that he soon discovered that she was a very agreeable and intelligent person, and she was not long in paying him the same compliment. By the time the sea voyage ended they were extremely good friends, and from what they saw of each other after landing in New York, and subsequently in Newport, simply confirmed and strengthened their first impressions. The result was that a private understanding existed between them which, in substance, amounted to an engagement, but they agreed to defer giving it that name, until after Arthur had presented himself in England and made formal application for her hand, which he intended doing in the immediate future. It will thus be seen that two of the members of Lord Grandwell's party were in a fair way to secure happiness by the formation of international ties; and it is a matter of regret that the earl should have been obliged to go home empty handed. If he had only fixed his choice on some person other than Miss Montague what a fortunate thing it would have been for him, and with what pleasure the writer would here record it; but alas! he must needs pick out the one person in the country who had no desire to become a countess.

It took Fred and Arthur, of course, only a short time, after they called upon the Grandwells, to find out the exact state of affairs existing between the earl and Miss Montague, at least so far as any public engagement was concerned; and Lady Constance expressed the opinion to Arthur that there was no foundation for the newspaper reports. When this was related to Tremaine he naturally felt much elated, and once more hope eternal abided within him. He argued pretty correctly that if the earl were returning home without being affianced to Miss Montague, it was not the former's fault, as judging by the state of his own feelings for her, he felt confident that the earl would not depart for home without having put the all-important question to her, and if he had received an answer in the affirmative there would be no object in keeping the affair secret.

From being loath at the start to call upon the Grandwells, Fred could not do too much for them when he learned that the newspaper reports of the engagement were unauthentic; and he and Arthur united in their efforts in giving them a suitable send-off. With the exception of Lord Grandwell's failure to win Miss Montague (which it must be admitted was quite serious for him) the visit of himself and party to the United States was attended with the greatest interest, and taken altogether proved to be a very enjoyable affair. They each expressed a warm desire to return again in the near future, and it may be taken for granted that Lady Constance and M. Rémiere were quite sincere in their protestations, as they both left landmarks behind; but as regards Lord Grandwell, he certainly had no wish to return to this country, at the time he uttered his polite remark, although it is more than probable that his mind will undergo a change in that respect, one of these days, after his sister has settled down on this side as the wife of Arthur D. Caldwell, Esq. As for Mrs. Montgomery she fully meant what she said; and when her services are required again as a chaperone she will be found on deck, ready for the occasion—God willing.

As our foreign friends will not appear again in these pages we will add our adieux to those of Messrs. Caldwell and Tremaine and wish them a *bon voyage*.

CHAPTER XI.

WHILE the Grandwells were in the city, Fred and Arthur had taken a couple of days off in order to be more at their service; and this, together with their short visit to Newport, was the only relaxation they had from business during the entire summer. With every day ushering in some new disaster in the business world, and the Stock Exchange barometer constantly making a new record in the fall of values, Wall street people were not disposed to go away for any length of time, not knowing where the financial lightning might strike during their absence. Arthur and Fred were beginning to feel the strain of overwork, and would have been glad of a few weeks' rest, but that feeling kept them from following their inclinations. Tremaine's firm now ranked as one of the leading brokerage houses, and very few firms on the "street" did a better paying business. Fred's appointment to the presidency of the Chattahooche Central had naturally brought his name prominently before the investing public, and in consequence had been the means of bringing his firm quite a number of new accounts. His business relations with Montague Bros. & Co., also continued to expand, so that taken altogether he and his father had their hands full and were more than satisfied with the result of their business venture.

The summer had been a trying one for all concerned, and every one was looking forward with pleasure to the beginning of a new year—feeling convinced that nothing but fresh disasters could be expected while any part of 1893 remained. The calling together of Congress in extra session for the purpose of repealing the purchasing clause in the Sherman silver law, had resurrected hope in the breasts of the people that better times were ahead; but the long-drawn fight in the senate, lasting several months before the bill was repealed, simply made matters worse, and long before the session ended many a person wished that the so-called "senatorial courtesy" might be side-tracked for the time being, and the overwhelming majority in the Upper House, in favor of repeal, be permitted to carry out the wishes of the people. If the bill had been promptly repealed, a great many financial and commercial disasters might have been averted, but distrust in the business world had become so deep-seated by the time the repealing act passed, it brought little or no immediate relief, and the drawing to a close of the year which had been set apart by the United States for celebrating the Four Hundredth Anniversary of Columbus' discovery of America, and of which so much had been expected, was eagerly awaited. Fred and Arthur had both received pressing invitations to visit the Montagues at Newport again, but other than passing an occasional Sunday there, they had been obliged to decline. The regular season was now over at that fashionable water resort, and the Montagues were back in their town house again where, it may be taken for granted, Mr. Tremaine (junior, of course) found time to call quite frequently. Miss Montague was quite interested in her railroad enterprise, and the president of the company naturally had to consult the chief stockholder and virtual owner of the road very often; this alone, therefore, afforded sufficient excuse for his frequent calls, outside of his intimate social relations with the family. With Lord Grandwell's departure Mrs. von Spraker had given up all hope of securing the earl for a nephew, and in consequence was more ready to acknowledge to herself that Mr. Tremaine possessed many fine traits of character and, taken altogether, was a man of more than ordinary attainments. It is proper to say that she had arrived at this conclusion none the less quickly for having had a short conversation with General Montague on the subject, who sounded Fred's praises without stint, and at the same time advised his sister to keep her hands off entirely if she wished to be free from trouble and disappointment. As Mrs. von Spraker by this time had found out that her niece had a strong will of her own, she was more than willing to follow the General's advice, and in doing so, she soon learned to appreciate Fred's good qualities which were quite apparent to any unprejudiced person who knew him well. Mrs. von Spraker's changed attitude toward him of course was very agreeable to Tremaine, who had often wondered at her frigid manner; he therefore redoubled his efforts to please her, with the result that she soon gave him a warmer reception even than he received from either the General or his niece, whenever he called. It will thus be seen that every day brought him nearer to the object he had in view.

In an earlier part of this book, in tracing Frederick Tremaine's character, in was clearly shown that he possessed an indomitable will which was not easily turned aside when once he had set his mind on any particular thing; with him it was a determination to succeed in everything he undertook to do, and as he was well equipped mentally and physically to meet and combat with any obstacles in his path, it will be seen that the chances of success were greatly in his favor. Thus far his short career had been eminently successful, and it was a marvel to most of his friends how he had managed to climb the slippery ladder of prosperity with nothing but his own resources to back him in such a comparatively short time. Some who did not know the man well ascribed it to luck, and the term "lucky dog" was often applied to him. The truth is that he owed his rapid advancement mostly to hard work and a persistency of purpose, which kept him constantly in harness ready to grasp everything which might legitimately come before him. He had not been in a position to go through one of the higher colleges; still that did not deter him from practically obtaining a collegiate education after he left school, by devoting his spare time to hard study; and thus it was with his whole life—his aim being to improve himself in every conceivable way. His sterling worth was what impressed every one who came into contact with him, and that, after all, was the principal reason of his success.

The reader, however, has discovered Mr. Tremaine's good qualities ere this, consequently there is no necessity for again calling attention to them. Besides, this narrative has already consumed much more space than originally intended, hence the necessity for reserving the remaining space for more important matter in which both Miss Montague and Mr. Tremaine are deeply interested. Before coming to that, however, another incident connected with Mr. Albert Stockholm's Wall street ventures will be related and a new chapter opened for that purpose.

CHAPTER XII.

The extrication of the Chattahooche Central Railroad from its financial difficulties, with Frederick Tremaine as its president, caused Mr. Stockholm to curse his broker more than once for having disposed of his stock—forgetting that he himself had authorized the sale, and that it was only owing to a fortunate circumstance he had managed to pull through with a comfortable balance left standing to his credit instead of a good sized debit. Like most people in his position, however, Mr. Stockholm would look at the matter in only one light, and that was, that he had been forced from the presidency of a railroad he had himself projected and built, and therefore robbed of his possessions—for that is what he styled it—and he intended by fair or by foul means to regain control. His inquiries concerning Fred's financial responsibility convinced him that his successor was not a man of much wealth, and he smiled grimly to himself as he mapped out a plan whereby he would knock the price of Chattahooche down to a point where somebody would have to unload. In accomplishing this he would not only be making money on the drop—for he intended putting out a line of shorts first—but in bringing about a decline he would pick up the long stock that came out, and it is needless to say he hoped that Tremaine's friends might be the ones to get frightened and unload. He imagined that Caldwell, in buying 75,000 shares from Goldbury, bought the stock for himself, and knowing that he was a professional room trader, he reasoned that Arthur would be apt to let his stock go if he thought there was any likelihood of the company getting into difficulty again. In order to convey that impression it was his intention to circulate, or cause to be circulated, numerous derogatory reports about the company, hoping thereby to injure its credit; and if necessary he would even go so far as to have some trumped-up suits brought against it. Having been its former president he of course was familiar with all its workings, and was therefore in a position to know its most vulnerable points. Having made all his arrangements Mr. Stockholm started in to carry out the dastardly attack outlined above. He and Mr. Goldbury had parted company some time before, owing to their quarrel over the sale of the former's securities, and Stockholm was now doing his business through another firm of the name of Janson, Pope & Co., whose senior partner, Edward Janson, was the board member.

Like the securities of all railroads which have recently been released from receivers' hands the Chattahooche Central stock and bonds had gone up considerably—the bonds now selling in the neighborhood of 95 and the shares at $30\frac{1}{2}$.

Mr. Stockholm regarded these figures as representing the full value of each, and even without any ulterior object in view he would have felt inclined to sell the shares short, for a turn, at least, and with the machinery he intended to employ to assist him in "bearing" them, he considered the risk infinitesimal. He accordingly instructed Mr. Janson to go into the Chattahooche crowd on the floor of the Exchange, and quietly put out as much of the stock as he could, without materially lowering the price, up to 5,000 shares, and the next day he would duplicate the order. Janson hesitated to go short, to such an extent, of a stock whose capital was not large, but relied on his client's statement that something would transpire within a few days which would undoubtedly hurt the company's financial standing considerably—intimating that several heavy suits were about to be brought, etc., which the company could not successfully defend.

Believing that Mr. Stockholm was telling the truth and knew what he was talking about, his broker went to the Exchange as instructed, and after considerable difficulty succeeded in working off 5,000 shares without lowering the price below 28¼, and the next day 5,000 additional shares were put out which forced the price down to 26. Mr. Stockholm felt highly elated at his seeming success, and endeavored to have his broker sell 5,000 shares more. Mr. Janson had found no difficulty in borrowing the stock for delivery on easy terms, but he felt nervous about going short any more, and informed his client that he did not care to increase his line. Mr. Stockholm, however, was not to be balked in the carrying out of his plans, which bid fair to be so successful; he therefore distributed his selling orders through nearly a dozen other houses on the "street," until he had out fully 25,000 shares. It never occurred to him that there was any danger of the stock being cornered, for in olden times, when he was president, he had often put that amount out and in each case had taken his stock back at a profit. He ought to have realized that the reins had changed hands, and that he was no longer able to fleece the public. He left that part of it out of his calculations, however, and never dreamed that he himself stood in danger of being fleeced. After having sold 25,000 shares short, as described above, he had his lawyer institute a number of suits against the company on various pretexts, in the names of several of his friends who were willing to be made tools of, and at the same time the "street" was flooded with all kinds of ugly rumors concerning the Chattahooche Central, until the impression prevailed in some quarters that the road would soon have to ask for a receiver again. If the company's backers had been weak-kneed people, and its securities less closely held, the chances are that Mr. Stockholm's bold scheme might have turned out as he had planned; but unfortunately for him the reverse was the case,

Before going further it should be stated that President Tremaine and his backers were fully cognizant of what was going on, and Fred had even gone out of his way to warn the brokers, in a friendly way, who were selling Chattahooche shares to desist. The brokers, however, only laughed, as did also Mr. Stockholm when Fred's words of warning were repeated to him.

General Montague felt quite confident that Stockholm was the real instigator of the suits, and that the unfounded rumors floating around were also started by him for the purpose of injuring the company's credit. He took quite readily to Caldwell's suggestion, therefore, to loan all the Chattahooche Central stock that was wanted, on easy terms, and when Stockholm got through selling (they felt convinced that the sales were for his account) to call in the stock they had loaned and make him cover on any terms they saw fit to impose. In this way they would teach him a much needed lesson. As the General practically held all of the capital stock of the Chattahooche Central Railroad for his niece, the reader will understand how easy it was to carry out Caldwell's suggestion. They even went so far as to allow the price of the stock to decline to 20, without offering any particular support, simply through their various brokers taking all the stock that was thrown on the market by Stockholm, who had, by this time, increased his short interest to 40,000 shares, nearly all of which had been taken by the General's brokers, besides a number of scattering lots let go by frightened holders. Stockholm's plan thus far had worked to perfection, but when the price of the stock had reached 20, he was informed by Mr. Janson that it seemed to be pegged at that figure, and advised him to cover his sales. Instead of following this advice, Stockholm immediately went to another broker's office and instructed him to smash the market at all hazards—even if he had to sell the whole capital stock. The broker to whom Stockholm issued this wild order was a young man by the name of Larkins, not over-bright, who had recently joined the Exchange and was therefore a bad hand to take charge of such an unlimited order. Mr. Stockholm, however, was getting desperate, and disposed to cast prudence to the winds; besides he realized that none of his other brokers would execute such an order in a stock like Chattahooche. He had purposely picked out young Larkins therefore, because of his inexperience, to deal what he considered would be a broadside cut; and he felt sanguine that this last bold move would bring out an avalanche of stock if young Larkins followed the instructions he had given him. The few orders the latter had previously been intrusted with were seldom for more than one or two hundred shares; he felt quite elated, therefore, as he stepped into the Stock Exchange, and the self-satisfied smile he wore boded no good to the unfortunate holders of Chattahooche Central. Going directly to that part of the Exchange where Chattahooche was traded in, he found a large number of brokers congregated there, including Tremaine and Caldwell. With a dignity befitting the occasion young Larkins asked, in the voice of a stentor, "What's Chattahooche?"

"Twenty bid; none offered," Tremaine quietly answered.

"None offered?" Larkins exclaimed. "Well I'll take care of that. Who wants any at 20?"

"I can use any part of a thousand at that figure," Tremaine answered.

"Sold the lot," Larkins said. "Want any more?"

"Oh, I can find a place for all you have got," Tremaine carelessly replied.

"A thousand at 20," Larkins yelled, and in this way he disposed of 5,000 shares without having broken the price even an eighth of one per cent.

At this juncture Caldwell good-naturedly sung out—"See here, Larkins, remember Dan Drew's words—'He who sells what isn't his'n, will sooner or later go to prison.'"

"You mind your own business, Caldwell," young Larkins rejoined. "I know what I am about."

"I don't think you do," Tremaine observed. "Take my advice and go back to your office and tell Mr. Stockholm you have cancelled his order; and if you wish I will call the 5,000 shares off which you have just sold to me at 20."

By this time half the brokers on the floor were crowded around the Chattahooche trading post, and excitement was beginning to run high. Tremaine's proposition was of course very generous, but Larkins had an idea that he was trying to crawl; so instead of accepting the offer he roared back, "You've got hold of the wrong man this time, Tremaine. You ought to have considered what you were about before you made the purchases. I refuse to let you off. You should understand that this is an Exchange for bona fide transactions, not for bluffs. If you can't take the stock, say so, and I will notify the chairman to sell it out under the rule."

"That's right, Larky," some of the brokers yelled, much amused; "don't let him off. Give him ten thousand more."

"Don't you worry about Larkins," that astute gentleman rejoined. "He is quite able to take care of himself." As if to prove the truth of his words he immediately offered 20,000 shares at 19¾.

"Tremaine is bidding 20 for the whole capital stock," Caldwell yelled. "Take my advice Larkins and quit."

"I don't want your advice nor any one else's," Larkins roared back. He was now in a white heat, owing to the jeers of the brokers. "You fellows can't bluff me for a cent, and I want you to understand it. If Tremaine is bidding 20 "—glaring fiercely at him—" I offer 20,000 shares at that figure."

With a shrug of his shoulders, as though deprecating the other's folly, but determined to keep the price at 20, Tremaine took the lot, and another and still another, before the insane Larkins realized what he was about. In fact but for the interference of one or two brokers who pulled him away from the crowd, the chances are that he would have followed out his client's instructions in literal earnest, and sold the whole capital stock short. When Larkins reached his office and reported to Mr. Stockholm that he had sold 65,000 shares at 20, the latter looked at him in speechless astonishment for a few moments, and then burst out laughing. When he had recovered sufficiently to speak he said —

"Of all the idiotic asses roaming around the world without a keeper, you are without exception the biggest coot of them all. Sold 65,000 shares at 20 did you? You must be crazy, man. Your name should be changed to 'Cosset' and a bell tied around your neck so that every one might know what an innocent you are." And again Mr. Stockholm burst out laughing. Presently, however, his mood changed and catching the unlucky Larkins by the throat, he hissed —

"You infernal villain, you are in league with that scoundrel Tremaine. I see through your game, but it won't work let me tell you. I repudiate the whole transaction," and picking his broker up bodily he threw him violently against a glass partition which shattered into a thousand pieces. All this took place in the broker's private office, and before his startled clerks made their appearance Stockholm had gone.

That night all the brokers who were borrowing Chattahooche Central stock were notified to return it and on the following day one of the most exciting scenes ever witnessed on the Exchange took place when Stockholm's brokers attempted to cover his short sales. From 20—the starting point—the price gradually soared up to 50 without bringing out any stock worth mentioning, and the situation looked rather startling for the brokers who had sold short for Stockholm, for it was apparent to them that the price could easily advance to par without bringing out any stock.

Tremaine and Caldwell had taken no hand in advancing the price, their instructions from General Montague being to do nothing one way or the other until he advised them. Mr. Janson and the other brokers who were caught in the net, had fairly beseeched Fred to let them cover, but to their anxious enquiries he could only say "I am very sorry indeed, but my principal has given me no selling orders; until I hear from him I can do nothing." He had been obliged to repeat this statement over and over again, and was beginning to wish that the General would send him the necessary selling orders, when presently a messenger handed him a note instructing him to make a private settlement with all who wished to do so at 50, and if any person refused the terms offered, to advance the price to par. When Fred made the terms known to the brokers they lost no time in accepting them, and each breathed more freely when the transactions were closed, notwithstanding that at the price paid, they would each figure as large sized creditors against Albert Stockholm, from whom they expected to get little or nothing. And in that respect it may be stated here that they were not disappointed, for the ex-president of Chattahooche Central left his creditors in the lurch, and they heard afterward that he had sailed for Europe under an assumed name, where, let us hope, he will remain for good, for the fewer Stockholms Wall street has the better it will be for all concerned.

Broker Larkins, whom Stockholm justly styled a cosset, was obliged to sell his seat in the Exchange and the story of how he smashed Chattahooche will long be remembered on the "street" as a huge joke, unparalleled in the history of the Exchange.

CHAPTER XIII.

Miss Montague had been kept fully informed of the events leading up to the scenes recorded in the last chapter, and her uncle and Tremaine had great difficulty in persuading her that the course adopted in dealing with a man like Stockholm, who resorted to all kinds of disreputable methods to gain his ends, was the proper one. She would fain have spared him, but her uncle was quite obdurate, and for once refused to be guided by her wishes, telling her the matter had now gone too far to recede, and Stockholm must suffer the consequences of his folly.

She watched the ticker in her uncle's study with the greatest interest and when the stock reached 50 she telephoned him that she would send selling orders to every broker on the "street" in his name, if he did not permit the shorts to cover their contracts at once. It was really this message that determined the General in sending word to Tremaine to settle at 50, and but for it the chances are that he would have permitted the stock to cross par, for he was much incensed at Stockholm's dastardly attempt to injure the company's credit, and was inclined to visit his sins on the heads of his brokers who were aiding him, in a measure, by selling the stock short for him. In crying quits at 50, when he had it in his power to force a settlement at double that figure, he considered that he had been very magnanimous, and the reader will doubtless concur in that opinion. The net profits from the deal—which were divided equally between the General, Caldwell and Tremaine—amounted to a trifle over $1,000,000, and would have been nearly three times as large but for Larkins' inability to settle. It will be seen, therefore, that the punishment meted out to Stockholm was quite severe and sufficient to keep his memory fresh on the subject for some years to come. That his brokers should have suffered pecuniary losses from his wrongdoing is a matter of regret, for they were in no way blameworthy. It affords a striking example, however, of how the unexpected sometimes happens, when a person sells something which he does not own or possess. Examples of this nature, however, are not of common occurrence on Wall street nowadays, for the reason, perhaps, that the watering-can has been the means of producing large supplies of floating stocks, thereby making it difficult to engineer and carry through a corner successfully. Still, as shown in the case of the Chattahooche Central, they do occur occasionally and when they do ,somebody is apt to get pinched.

Frederick Tremaine had no idea General Montague intended giving him a third interest in the Chattahooche anti-short deal; he was completely surprised, therefore, when a messenger from Montague Bros. & Co. handed him a note informing him that in compliance with instructions received from General Montague they begged to enclose their check for $340,000, payable to his (Frederick Tremaine's) order, and asking for an acknowledgment of the same by bearer. Fred had not the slightest idea for what purpose the check was intended, and was on the point of asking the young man who brought it, if he could enlighten him, when that individual—as if divining his thoughts—produced another letter from his pocket, which Fred found upon opening, was from General Montague, explaining that he had directed his firm to send him a check for his share of the profits in the Chattahooche deal, and congratulating him on the way he had managed the affair. Being a cool-headed and practical young man, he promptly wrote a letter of acknowledgment to Montague Bros. & Co., and also a letter of thanks to the General, and then quietly handed the check in to his cashier for deposit and credit, as though the transaction was an everyday occurrence. His outward composure, however, was in sharp contrast to his feelings within, for the thought immediately occurred to him that he was now in a position, sufficiently independent to enable him to ask Miss Montague for her hand in marriage without laying himself open to the charge of being a fortune hunter. His sensitiveness on this point had deterred him from making her a formal offer long before this, for his independent nature shrunk at the bare thought that she or her relatives might misconstrue his motives and think he was actuated in the slightest degree by the knowledge that she was the possessor of an enormous fortune. This stumbling-block was now partially removed, and he resolved that, come what may, he would find out what the fates had in store for him without further delay. That evening he occupied a seat in the Montague opera box, but, of course, made no attempt there to acquaint Miss Montague with the subject that was uppermost in his thoughts; he found out from her, however, that she had no engagement for the following evening and gave her to understand that he would then call upon her as he had something important to communicate. Miss Montague took it for granted that the something was in connection with railroad matters, and once or twice during the evening reverted to the subject, but Fred put her off by saying that he would be in a better position on the morrow to impart to her fuller particulars.

Tremaine was not prone to nervousness and made it a rule not to allow thoughts of his private affairs to obtrude themselves during business hours. He is to be excused, however, if he did not strictly enforce this rule the following day, especially as it cost him $250 for momentarily departing from it, having executed an order to buy a thousand shares of St. Paul by selling it instead—a mistake that is sometimes made by careless brokers, but one Tremaine had never before been guilty of—and which he berated himself soundly for making.

Fred had plenty of confidence in his own business

abilities, having put them successfully to the test in numerous instances, but when it came to an affair of the heart, such as he now had in hand, (not that he had ever had much experience in that direction) he was apt to underrate his powers of attraction and gave himself infinitely less credit in that respect than he really deserved, especially with a girl of Miss Montague's stamp of character, who considered natural intelligence almost before anything else —believing that if a person possessed that quality to a large extent under ordinary circumstances he would be apt to go in for everything of an ennobling nature rather than the reverse. This was certainly true in Tremaine's case, at least, and had done more to win Miss Montague's regard and (I was going to add affection, but that point has not yet been fully determined) than anything else, although he was not deficient by any means in his personal appearance which, as has already been explained to the reader, was decidedly prepossessing. The feeling of uncertainty, whether Miss Montague really cared for him in the light of a suitor, however, did not make him hesitate in the least to speedily put the matter to a test, now that he had made up his mind to do so, and Miss Montague certainly could not accuse him of being tardy when he presented himself at her residence in the evening. Mention has already been made of the fact that Mrs. von Spraker's feelings toward Termaine had undergone a change, and instead of placing obstacles nowadays in the way of his suit, as formerly, she did all she could to further it, and was really beginning to look upon him as a *protégé* of her own. One of the cardinal principles of General Montague's life was to avoid meddling in other people's affairs; he was very careful therefore not to show a preference for or against any of the numerous suitors for his niece's hand, feeling confident that she was quite able to take care of herself. There is no question, however, that Fred was a prime favorite of the General's, and if he had been called upon to choose for her, he would unhesitatingly have given him the first call. It will be understood from this that Fred's course was to be one of clear sailing, as far as the General and his sister were concerned, and he had not been slow to recognize that as a point in his favor; at the same time he realized that in a matter of so much importance to herself Miss Montague was not likely to be influenced by other people's preferences, choosing rather to be governed solely by her own feelings in the matter.

Owing to Mrs. von Spraker's good offices, Tremaine had no difficulty in securing a private audience with her niece a few minutes after he arrived, without going to the formality of asking for it—Mrs. von Spraker leaving them alone together with the remark that she detested business in all its forms, and she would go down and talk to Charles (the General was in his study smoking) while they were discussing it. She had several times previous to this left them in a similar manner—her departure therefore occasioned no surprise. It, however, brought forth a comment from her niece who said, laughingly —

"Poor Aunt Charlotte, I believe she does not overstate it when she says she detests business in all its forms. She of course leaves everything to Uncle Charles appertaining to her business affairs—or at least tries to—and whenever he brings home a paper for her to sign—insisting that she must first read it over carefully—she actually gets a headache in trying to understand its meaning. She displays so much intelligence in dealing with other matters I cannot make it out. I suppose, however, that her want of understanding, in respect to business matters, is due almost entirely to the fact that she has never had any business experience or training."

Fred was very glad that her thoughts strayed off in this fashion, rather than to the special object of his visit. He had told her at the opera that he had something of importance to communicate; he was afraid, therefore, that the first question she would put to him, after her aunt left the room, would be in reference to it. Like most people with an important subject in hand, Fred had given considerable thought to the matter before him, and was prepared, at the proper moment, to tell her in a few well chosen words what he wished to say, and then to use any amount of argument necessary to carry his point. He, of course, did not want to do this in an abrupt manner, and was thankful that Miss Montague herself had relieved him of the necessity for so doing. Moreover he was quite willing to discuss her aunt's business qualifications,—or rather lack of them—until the subject ran dry, feeling that time gained would suit his purpose better than time saved. He answered her remarks therefore by saying —

"No doubt that is the reason, Miss Montague. You ought to be thankful that you have gained an insight into business matters so early in life."

"And do you imagine that I do not appreciate the pains and trouble you have taken to gain me that insight?" she asked. "You have taught me everything; and indeed I *am* thankful, for you have enabled me to combine duty with pleasure."

Here was the opportunity Tremaine was waiting for; he answered quickly then—regardless of the fact that the words he used were not in the little speech he had intended making—by saying earnestly —

"Not everything, Miss Montague. There is one important element I have left out."

"What's that?" she asked, in surprise, more at his manner than at the words he used.

"How to love," he answered; "and that above everything else in the world is of the most importance to me. Is there no way I can teach you that, Helen?"

One glance at her blushing cheeks and the light that shone from her eyes was sufficient to convince him that her heart was his even before she murmured,

"You have taught me that also."

With the recording of this last scene the story of "Fortuna," the American Goddess of Fortune ends. Like the mythological Hellenic heroine, "from her hand were derived riches and poverty, happiness and misery."

FINIS.

www.ingramcontent.com/pod-product-compliance
Lightning Source LLC
Chambersburg PA
CBHW020824230426
43666CB00007B/1086